SENSE AND DELUSION

STUDIES IN
PHILOSOPHICAL PSYCHOLOGY

Edited by
R. F. HOLLAND

SENSE AND DELUSION

by
İLHAM DİLMAN
and
D. Z. PHILLIPS

LONDON
ROUTLEDGE & KEGAN PAUL
NEW YORK: HUMANITIES PRESS

First published 1971
by Routledge & Kegan Paul Ltd
Broadway House, 68–74 Carter Lane
London, EC4V 5EL
Printed in Great Britain by
Richard Clay (The Chaucer Press), Ltd
Bungay, Suffolk
© *İlham Dilman & D. Z. Phillips 1971*
ISBN 0 7100 6935 9

TABLE OF CONTENTS

76196

PREFACE

THIS book grew out of discussions we have had since 1966. These discussions started in a rather informal manner and not until later did we begin to put things down on paper in a more formal way and reply to each other in writing. These papers finally culminated in the chapters of this book, with the exception of the first chapter which was the starting point of our discussions.

The paths which our discussions have followed are not, of course, the only possible ones which could have resulted from the topics under consideration. Thus, we do not claim this to be a comprehensive treatment of all the questions connected with our field of interest.

We have both found the exchange out of which the chapters in this book grew profitable. We were continually forced to revise what we had said previously and attend to new questions. Many of our disagreements were resolved during our discussions, but whatever our agreements and disagreements may have been, we felt all along that we were speaking on the same wave-length.

The paper 'Life and Meaning' was published in *Philosophy*, October 1965, and the Postscript to it is a revised version of a paper that was published in

Religious Studies, vol. 3. We are grateful to the editors of these journals for allowing this material to be reprinted here.

We are extremely grateful for the contributions and criticisms of colleagues, students and friends who joined in the discussion from time to time. We are particularly grateful to H. O. Mounce, Rush Rhees, Meirlys Owens, R. F. Holland, Peter Winch and D. M. Evans for their helpful suggestions.

İlham Dilman and D. Z. Phillips

CHAPTER 1

LIFE AND MEANING

İlham Dilman

PEOPLE sometimes ask whether their lives are meaningful or not, whether or not their lives add up to anything. Sometimes they also ask whether life as such is meaningful or not. These are not unconnected questions. Still they are not questions which everyone asks himself. Nor do we always readily recognize what one who asks these questions wants to know. There are some people who will not even find such questions sensible. Some will regard them not as questions but simply as symptoms of something having gone wrong somewhere. Thus in the Diary of the Student Kostya Ryabtsev we find the following words:

The Editor of *Katushka* raises the question, 'What do we live for?' Perhaps he wants to get into farflung discussions of philosophy. Perhaps, also, he is seized by a fear of the insignificance of human life. If the former is the case, all right. If the latter should be the case, that would be bad. For this reason: 'Living in order to live' is the only answer to the question, no matter how strange and one-sided it may sound. The whole meaning of life is life itself, the process of living. In order to comprehend the meaning of life one must, first of all, love life, must become completely submerged in it. Only then will one comprehend the meaning of life, will one understand what one lives for. Life—in contradistinction to all man has created—is something that requires no theory. Whoever is able to function in life will need no theory of life.[1]

The view is, I think, that such questions would not arise unless something went wrong—here described as 'the inability to function in life'. But, whether that is a happy description or not, even if it were true that such questions do not arise except under certain circumstances, however described, it still would not follow that they were not genuine questions. It would also be wrong to suggest that they always arise in the same way and for the same sort of reasons.

There are occasions when one asks what makes a certain person's life meaningful. Here one has in mind the various activities, concerns and preoccupations that make up the tissue of his life, and one is wondering what he finds in them. Perhaps one wants to learn something from such a person's life. Or it may be that one doesn't feel one would find anything much in that sort of life and wonders what anyone else can. One may wonder what sort of person one must be, what sort of attitude to life one must have, what sort of view of it one must take, to want to lead that sort of life and to get anything out of it. Here one will seek to understand the person in question.

Sometimes it seems to one that there is not much meaning in another person's life though one knows that the person himself doesn't think so. Here one may be inclined to attribute this appearance to one's own short-sightedness and arrogance and to make what the

[1] Quoted by Wilhelm Reich in his book *The Sexual Revolution*.

person himself thinks and says the criterion of whether
there is meaning in his life or not. Yet it may well be a
mistake to follow this inclination. Could one not, in all
humility, say to another person, 'If I know you at all,
if you are the sort of person I think you are, you are
really wasting your life and you don't like it yourself.
You don't get much out of the life you lead, you don't
put much into it. The way you spend your time must
seem rather futile and pointless to you, however unwilling you may be to recognize it'? Socrates may have
talked to Alcibiades along these lines. As Alcibiades
puts it in the *Symposium*: 'He compels me to realise
that I am still a mass of imperfections and yet
persistently neglect my own true interests by engaging
in public life. So *against my real inclination* I stop up
my ears and take refuge in flight . . .' (Penguin Classics,
pp. 101–2, *i.m.*). But, of course, one's suspicions may
be unfounded, he may not be the sort of person one
thought he was. Or one may have dismissed the way
of life as meaningless without regard to the person
whose life it is. What one should have said was: 'To
me that way of life would be meaningless. I couldn't
live that way.' But this is not to say that the other
person's life is meaningless.

So our idea that if a person thinks that his life is
meaningful then we cannot have reason to think
otherwise is false though it contains an important
truth. That truth is that we cannot separate a life
from the person whose life it is and judge the life by
our own personal standards—standards that we apply
to our own life. However, it does not follow that
there are not perfectly good standards for us to appeal
to in judging another person's life. There are—namely,
those of the other person. The only way to discover

these is to study the person and the life he lives. But though they are personal, this does not mean that they are not objective in the sense that other people can use them as well as he. They can. It is because others can use them that it is possible for another person to point out to him what he has failed to recognize. If this were not so we could not distinguish between appearance and reality here. My point is that we do.

One could say, therefore, that if the life that a person leads is genuinely meaningful to him then it must be a meaningful life whatever others may think of that sort of life. If, on the other hand, one suspects that it is not a meaningful life then, whether one's suspicions are well founded or not, what one is suspecting is that it does not really mean very much to the person whose life it is, whether he recognizes this himself or not. If this is the case, both his life and his personality will bear marks of it. Such marks alone may then lead one to wonder about the meaning of a man's life even though one does not know the man very well. However, it is easy to miss this out even when one knows the man well, or to recognize it and yet fail to convey it to another person. But the reverse is equally true sometimes. Consider the following conversation:

'And I think Kay and I are pretty happy. We've always been happy.'

Bill lifted up his glass and put it down without drinking.

'Would you mind saying that again?' he asked.

'I don't see what's so queer about it. Taken all in all, Kay and I have really been happy.'

'All right', Bill said gently. 'Just tell me how you and Kay have been happy.'

Bill had a way of being amused by things which I could not understand.

'It is a little hard to explain', I said. 'It's like taking a lot of numbers that don't look alike and that don't mean anything until you add them all together.'

I stopped, because I hadn't meant to talk to him about Kay and me.

'Go ahead', Bill said. 'What about the numbers?' And he began to smile.

'I don't know why you think it's so funny', I said. 'All the things that two people do together, two people like Kay and me, add up to something. There are the kids and the house and the dog and all the people we have known and all the times we've been out to dinner. Of course, Kay and I do quarrel sometimes but when you add it all together, all of it isn't as bad as the parts of it seem. I mean, maybe that's all there is to anybody's life.'

Bill poured himself another drink. He seemed about to say something and checked himself. He kept looking at me.[1]

The question about the meaning of another's life arises sometimes from a wish to learn from how this person lives, and sometimes from a failure to see the meaning that another finds in his life. It is, then, a challenge or a request for what is not apparent to be made plain. Here one wishes to improve or deepen one's understanding of a person's life. One may, however, come to be increasingly concerned with what it is that gives meaning to anybody's life. Of course one may still wish to learn something that will make a difference to one's life. But it may be that one is less concerned to understand a particular life or to modify one's own, more concerned with the nature of the

[1] *H. M. Pulham Esq.*, by John P. Marquand.

relationship between any life and the meaning it has for the person whose life it is. One is then concerned with the notion of meaningfulness as applied to a person's life: What is claimed about a person and the life he leads when his life is said to be meaningful? It must be remembered that here the term 'meaningful' is used to rule out the suggestion of some or all of its recognized antitheses. I should say that the positive word is used only in this way.[1] So to understand what might be meant when a person's life is said to be meaningful we have to understand what constitutes loss of meaning. In *The Death of Ivan Ilych* Tolstoy has given us an excellent study of this question to which I shall return.

Impressed by the extent to which people deceive themselves about their lives, by how little what they do really comes from them, by how much of it may be imitation, one may wish to know what distinguishes a genuinely meaningful life from one that is only apparently meaningful. One has come to recognize that it is not as easy to distinguish between them as one had thought. It may happen that the more one gives one's thoughts to the question the more insurmountable one's difficulty becomes. Forces are at work here which we are familiar with in more purely *a priori* philosophical reflection. Here too, as when one is concerned with knowledge, verification, truth, beauty and goodness, one may end up by questioning the very reality of the distinction that is central to one's inquiry: Is there really a difference between a life that is meaningful and one that is not? Is there a meaningful life? One has reached a position of philosophical scepticism.

This may lead one to ask what makes it possible for

[1] With acknowledgments to Professor Austin.

human life to have a meaning. What gives it that dimension? We can compare what is being asked here with the question philosophers have asked about the meaning and intelligibility of discourse. Not only are these questions similar in kind, but they also run into each other. For, as Wittgenstein has shown us, there are far-reaching connections between what makes discourse possible and what makes possible the kind of life that has a meaning, the kind of life that can lose its meaning. Here then the desire to understand the difference between a meaningful and a meaningless life seems to have led to the desire to understand the conditions which must be fulfilled if such a distinction is to be possible.

In her book *L'Enracinement* Simone Weil writes: 'A human being has roots by virtue of his real, active and natural participation in the life of a community which preserves in living shape certain particular treasures of the past and certain particular expectations for the future. This participation is a natural one, in the sense that it is automatically brought about by place, conditions of birth, profession and social surroundings. Every human being needs to have multiple roots. It is necessary for him to draw wellnigh the whole of his moral, intellectual and spiritual life by way of the environment of which he forms a natural part.' I should say that man's moral, intellectual and spiritual life is *not even conceivable* in the absence of the ways of living in which he participates—ways of living many of which *could* not have developed apart from language.

She says that when a man loses his roots then his spirit perishes. Wittgenstein writes: 'Can only those hope who can talk? Only those who have mastered the use of a language. That is to say, the phenomena of hope are modes of this complicated form of life.' When he speaks of the relations between forms of life and modes of discourse he has in mind a two-way dependence. Thus not only does he say that only those who can talk can hope, but also that 'it is essential to mathematics that its signs should also be used in civil life'. Without that use outside, without this weaving into many strands of life, mathematics he would say becomes a 'wallpaper pattern'. Just as if we imagined human beings taking part *only* in one form of activity we would reduce them to mere puppets.[1]

The concepts of meaning and understanding have many dimensions. Thus, for instance, we speak of the meanings of words such as we may look up in a dictionary. Also we ask: Now what did he mean by that? You cannot satisfy yourself on that point by consulting a dictionary, though if you did not understand the language in which he spoke you could not even begin to understand him. We also speak of understanding a person's actions. So we say: I do not understand what he is up to. In some ways this is similar to failing to understand what he meant by what he said. Sometimes we say of a person that he is not behind his words, that they do not carry any conviction. One could say that there is not much to understand in them, in the sense in which we may wish to understand what someone is trying to convey. There he has something to say, here he doesn't. In extreme cases we speak of meaningless chatter. Sometimes we also say that what a person is doing has not much sense for him, that his heart is not in it, that he is only

[1] I should like to acknowledge an enormous debt to Mr Rush Rhees for my reading of Wittgenstein.

going through the motions. It is not an accident that here too we use the concepts of sense and meaning. Just as a person may speak and yet have nothing to say, so may a person do various things without putting much of himself into the doing of them and so without finding much sense in what he does. If he doesn't find much sense in what he is doing that means that it doesn't matter much whether he does it or not. Just as if my utterances have no sense it makes very little difference what I utter. Having no purpose and interests, no heart to do anything, and having nothing to say—these go together.

Writing about how learning to speak differs from learning to play a game Mr Rhees writes:

> When he (the child) can speak we may be delighted because 'He can say things himself now—not just repeat.' But what is important is that he can *say* things: not that he can construct new sentences—as it were in an exercise. If he can speak, he has got something to tell you.

If we leave this out, he says, then we have left out 'the most important thing'. A little way down he goes on:

> Not all speech is conversation, of course, but I do not think there would be speech or language without it. ... Now one reason why a conversation is not like playing a game together is that the point of the various moves and counter-moves is within the game. Whereas we may learn from a conversation and from what is said in it. Generally each of us brings something to the conversation too: not as he might bring skill to the game, but just in having something to say ('Wittgenstein's Builders', *Arist. Soc. Proc.* 1959–60, pp. 181–2).

B

So having something to say belongs with the idea of speaking. Without it a person's words would degenerate into meaningless chatter. But still it is important that his words are in a language that others understand. The possibility of their degenerating into meaningless chatter rests on that. Although there are differences, similar considerations apply to a man's life, his actions and activities losing their sense. That possibility too depends on their being variants of ways of living and forms of activity which others take part in. That is the point, I think, of bringing in the notions of uprootedness and alienation into an account of the conditions wherein a man's life is said to have lost its meaning.

When a man's life does lose its meaning he will no longer be able to derive intellectual and spiritual nourishment from the treasures of the culture and tradition (what Socrates was speaking of as 'laws' in the *Crito*) to which he owes his whole being. Without that nourishment he will no longer be able to relate himself to others, he will lose all understanding of himself and others. His soul will perish. He might say: 'I don't know who I am or what I am.' I am not speaking of causes and effects here, but of a complex transformation and of the way its various features hang together and depend on each other for their very identity.

I have been speaking about the question whether a person's life has meaning or not and I shall return to it a little later. But there are other questions which people have also asked, different from and yet connected with the ones mentioned: 'Has life any meaning?', 'What is the meaning of life?' One may ask the latter question not because life seems meaningless but

because one wishes to understand better what makes
it meaningful. That is one may wish to reflect on what
one already knows and seek to articulate it. Or again
one's question may come from one's dissatisfaction
with answers given or suggested by others—answers
to be found in accounts of the human condition given
by philosophers, religious and literary writers. One
may wish to protest: That is not what gives meaning
to life; that is not the meaning of life! But if not, then
what is? Or, one may wish to meet arguments de-
signed to show that everything is absurd and pointless, and that if it seems otherwise this is no more than
a fond illusion. One may be sure that this conclusion
must be wrong and yet find it very difficult to detect
or show what is wrong with the argument.

The best treatment I know of this question is com-
pressed in a few paragraphs in a broadcast talk that
Professor Wisdom gave called 'What is there in Horse
Racing?'[1] In that talk Wisdom was concerned to show
where the excitement that people find in horse racing
comes from, how this may vary from one individual to
another, and what it is bound up with. He was concerned to show that 'getting things out of focus' may
indeed make the whole thing seem absurd, but that
even when this isn't the case misguided reflection may
make it seem as if one's pleasure and excitement must
rest on an illusion. For one may easily come to ask:
'What is it but a matter of whether one horse has his
head in front of another?' Wisdom shows, with one or
two strokes of the brush, how very much more it is
than that. He writes: 'With some things it is easy to
realise that there is more in them than meets the eye or
can be put into words—music, poetry, mathematics.'

[1] Printed in *The Listener*, 10 June 1954.

But even here, he points out, muddled critics ask 'What purpose do they serve?' We are confident we can meet the critics' complaint here. However, it is easy to lose this confidence in the case of smaller things. 'Some things seem small, seem easy, and seem to have little in them, and then, if we give time to them, we feel bound to answer "What is there in them?" ' We are intimidated too by our inability to set out in words what makes them worthwhile. No doubt some people are better at this than others. Thinking of the skilled critic who sets out to put into words what there is in *Hamlet*, Wisdom says: 'But, however skilled he were, I am sure that much of what makes "Hamlet" "Hamlet" will run between his fingers, much of it anyway. And this is no less true of small things.'

In the case of horse racing, as in other things, cro- quet or conversation, writes Wisdom, 'human per- sonality finds expression; human personalities are joined whether for good or not'. Of course, it is not a matter of whether one horse has his head in front of another. 'That small incident (says Wisdom) is the last move in a long game which began before the colt was born. . . . It is a game with something of the flavour of life itself.'

Wisdom was speaking on the occasion of the Derby and was concerned with horse racing. But he was also thinking of the bigger question about life. He said, 'It is interesting to notice that the same argu- ments by which clever persons sometimes represent to us as worthless things much bigger than horse racing are also to be used in this smaller matter.' However, there is a more important connection between the two questions. It is not merely that they are similar in kind and that similar arguments can be made to bear on them. For, as Wisdom is concerned to show, the quality which life has for us rests on what we are able to find in these smaller things. He writes:

Behind the words 'What is the *purpose* of racing?' lies the innuendo that if it doesn't serve a purpose it is no good and waste of time and absurd. But the innuendo is itself absurd. For these things, such as surgical operations, or hewing coal, or what you will, which do serve a purpose, do so only because they are means to things which are worth while in themselves, worth while not because of any purpose they serve but because of what is in them—health and well-being before a warm fire, playing with a friend a game of draughts or ludo, if you like.

However, it is not only the difficulty of putting into words what makes life meaningful, the difficulty of grasping how much more there is in almost any part of it than meets the eye, and the power which certain misconceived questions have on our thoughts, that may make it seem that the meaning of life must be an illusion. This may become more than a logical or philosophical conclusion. One may be convinced that it is an illusion which one has come to lose. The whole of life, in one's deepest apprehension of it, may collapse into a farce or absurdity—'full of sound and fury, signifying nothing'. As Celia puts it in Eliot's *The Cocktail Party*:

'. . . it isn't that I *want* to be alone,
But that everyone's alone—or so it seems to me.
They make noises, and think they are talking to each other;

> They make faces, and think they understand each
> other.
> And I'm sure that they don't. Is that a delusion?'

The claim, the vision here, is one that has much more than one's own life as its object. Yet it is a vision that comes out of one's own life. Certainly things have been thrown out of focus, but also some things have come into focus. That is why it is not altogether a delusion. Besides, one may have lost an illusion about one's own life, and what one perceives there may be very far from being the result of a delusion.

What view of life must one take, then, to see no point or meaning in it? One may form an exaggerated vision of the selfishness in men. This may give all their concerns and preoccupations an appearance of self-centred pettiness. All human contact may take on the guise of mutual exploitation, love dwindle into a fetish and an addiction. In the end, even reason and understanding may come to be excluded by the surroundings given them and become illusions that cover something different. Or one may come to see life against the background of impending death. As if two people playing chess were to be told that someone would come along and upset the pieces before the end of the game. It is understandable that they should feel that they may as well pack up—since it makes very little difference now what moves they make. I am not, of course, saying that all those who carry on and who manage to find a point in their lives are oblivious of this. Some are not; and though it does make a difference, it does not make *this* difference. A psychoanalyst may well illuminate here why it makes just this difference with this person.

What is interesting is the penetrating realism that so often goes with such despairing scepticism. One wants to understand how such a sceptical vision comes from the experiences of the person in question. One wishes to grasp the nature of the connection between the vision and the determinants of the experiences. For whether such a vision be penetrating or delusive it sits as deep in the person as his most intimate experiences. It may be, for instance, that such a person is not able to find any love in his heart for anyone. Or it may be that his ability to be sincere is poisoned at its very roots by an extreme concern for personal gain of whatever sort. One may appreciate that this will twist his life into a meaningless pattern, but ask why it should twist his very conception of life. Of course it may not. A person could say, quite sincerely, that the meaning has gone out of his life, but that he does not see life as meaningless. He may feel estranged and excluded from other people without thinking that they are labouring under an illusion. But sometimes his whole understanding of life will be affected.

In Ivan Ilych (in Tolstoy's story) we have the case of a man who recognizes on his death-bed that his life has come to nothing. He doesn't doubt that life has any meaning, but he recognizes that his had none. The recognition is retrospective and there is no time now to alter that. He has only to prepare for death.

What is it that Ivan realizes in realizing that his life has come to nothing, that it has been meaningless? What is it that he has rejected and lost? How and why has he rejected it, and why does it make this difference to him?

Tolstoy tells us about Ivan's associations and friendships, about his marriage, his work and ambitions. In his work he is ambitious to climb up, he is anxious to be well thought of by others, particularly those whose position in the social ladder he aspires to. He adopts their conceptions, their values, their ways, and he is extremely anxious to keep up appearances. The peculiarity of Ivan's social climb is that it takes him further and further away from himself and deadens him. It is not the case that as he grows older and more mature new experiences mould and modify his personality; it is rather that what he adopts never becomes his. The life he leads remains alien to him. By this I mean that the wishes and needs that steer his course and which find fulfilment in it express only part of his personality. Also there is something fake about them. He gradually stifles and loses touch with other facets of his personality. As Tolstoy puts it: 'All the passions of childhood and youth had passed away, not leaving serious traces.' On his death-bed reviewing the course of his life Ivan finds that 'according as he went back, there was more and more of life. There was more also of excellence in life, and more of life itself. And the two were confounded.'

I said that there is one aspect of Ivan's personality which seeks the way he actually lives and finds expression and gratification in it. I have in mind mainly the stuff of his driving ambition. Superficially its main characteristic is vanity. But Tolstoy shows us a new aspect of it: 'The consciousness of his power, and the possibility of tempering it, furnished for him the chief interest and attractiveness of his new office.' 'The consciousness of his power of ruining anyone whom he might wish to ruin . . . delighted him.' So we see that exercising power over other people, injuring them, has a secret fascination for Ivan and constitutes an aspect of his ambition. Tolstoy shows us how much this infects and desiccates his relationships, particularly his relation with his wife. He can only guard against his wish to take from and triumph over others by avoiding the give and take of human intercourse: 'It was necessary that he should tolerate no relations with people except on an official basis.'

It is not difficult to see that the theme of depression and the fear of it runs through the whole of Ivan's life. Tolstoy tells us that being 'deeply in the dumps' is 'a thing which Ivan Ilych dreaded above all'. This brings to light a new side to the nature of Ivan's ambition and activities. We begin to see how much in many of his activities he tries to keep depression at bay, and guilt as well: 'In the country, relieved of his official duties, Ivan Ilych for the first time felt not only irksomeness, but insupportable anguish.' However, staving off depression becomes progressively more difficult. At first the consciousness of depression revolves around his illness. But later Ivan begins to recognize the source of his anguish: ' "The vermiform appendix! the kidney!" he said to himself. "The trouble lies, not in the blind intestine, not in the kidney . . . but in life . . . and death!" '

Ivan now begins to see in those around him something of what he has been like himself: 'Schwartz especially irritated him with his jocularity, his lively ways and his *comme-il-faut*-ness, reminding Ivan Ilych of himself as he had been ten years before.' Tolstoy brilliantly portrays how little Ivan's family and friends now care for him, how much they 'surround him with a lie', and how they keep away from an appreciation of his situation. Behind this, behind their petty egoisms, is fear and terror. All this illuminates Ivan's past life: 'He saw in them himself, all that for which he had lived; and he saw clearly that all this was wrong, all this was a terrible, monstrous lie, concealing both life and death.'

Now he begins to interrogate himself, to search his soul:

> ... he heard, not a voice speaking with sounds, but the voice of his soul, the tide of his thoughts, arising in him.
>
> 'What do you need? What do you need?' he said to himself. 'What? Freedom from suffering. To live', he replied.
>
> 'To live? how live?' asked the voice of his soul.
>
> 'Yes, to live as I used to live—well, pleasantly.'
>
> 'How did you live before when you lived well and pleasantly?' asked the voice.
>
> And he began to call up in his imagination the best moments of his pleasant life. But, strangely enough, all these best moments of his pleasant life seemed to him absolutely different from what they had seemed then—all, except the earlier remembrances of his childhood. . . . But the person who had enjoyed that pleasant existence was no more; it was as if it were the remembrance of someone else.
>
> As soon as the period began, which had produced the present *he*, Ivan Ilych, all the pleasures which seemed such then, now in his eyes dwindled away, and changed into something of no account, and even disgusting.
>
> And the farther he departed from infancy, and the nearer he came to the present, so much the more unimportant and dubious were the pleasures.
>
> This began in the law-school. There was still something even then which was truly good; then there was gaiety, there was friendship, there were hopes. . . .
>
> My marriage. . . . And this dead service, and these

labours for money; and thus one year, and two, and
ten, and twenty,—and always the same thing. And
the longer it went, the more dead it became.

It is as if all the time I were going down the
mountain, while thinking that I was climbing it. So
it was. According to public opinion, I was climbing the
mountain; and all the time my life was gliding away
from under my feet. . . .

Tolstoy's story is fairly brief, of course, and in all
that is conveyed in it there is much that is merely
suggested. But it gives a very profound portrait of a
man whose life has been meaningless though he has
failed to recognize this himself. It shows us what the
recognition of this comes to.

If I were asked to sum up in a few words what it is
that made Ivan Ilych's life meaningless I would draw
attention to three related features that it has. First, I
would mention its alienated character. By this I mean
that it is not really his life; not the life he would live if
he were himself, if he were true to himself. This notion
of not being oneself, not being true to oneself, is a
difficult notion which raises many interesting philosophical questions which I cannot go into now. I spoke
of there being something fake about some of the wishes
and needs that seem to be central to Ivan's life. What
I meant was that he would not have needed to achieve
a great deal of what he strived after if he had not
wanted desperately to avoid facing the anguish and
depression in his heart. One could say, too, that he
did not live according to his own values. Again this
raises difficulties which I do not have the space to
discuss. It is no wonder that Ivan was not really
interested in a great deal of what he spent his time on,
not for itself, and that he found very little fulfilment

in it. Though he seems to have managed pretty well to achieve this false security and assurance it seems to have got between him and the world at large preventing any genuine commerce with it. So, secondly, I would mention the negative character of Ivan's life, by which I mean that a great deal of it is directed by the need to stave off something—fear, guilt, depression. Thirdly, I would mention its destructive character and the absence of what would mitigate whatever makes for this destructiveness—or rather not its absence but its failure to be operative. It is here, I think, that is to be found the source of the sense of isolation, the inability to give and receive love, the inability to care, and at an extreme the absolute indifference characteristic of those who cannot find any meaning in life, at least in their own.

In conclusion let me summarize: I started with the question 'Do the words "Has life any meaning?", "Has my life any meaning?", "Has his life any meaning?" put genuine questions?' I have tried to show that they do and that there is more than one question which may be asked in these words. I have maintained that it is certainly possible here to distinguish between appearance and reality. When we claim a person's life to be meaningless we are not claiming that *we* find that sort of life meaningless but that *he* finds it so, although it may appear to him otherwise.

While it is important to emphasize that the words 'Has my life any meaning?' and 'Has his life any meaning?' can put the same question, it is equally important to recognize that my relation to what I am questioning when I use the first-person form of words is entirely different from my relation to what I am questioning when I use the second- or third-person form of words. One of the differences comes out in the fact that while I may fail to recognize that my life has become meaningless, deceive myself about it, if it seems that my life has become meaningless, this is at least in part a symptom of recognition. It is never simply a mistake. Thus the question asked in the first-person is almost always part of the syndrome we have been concerned with. In the case of 'Has life any meaning?' this is equally so on *some* occasions. This is, I think, the truth in the passage that I quoted at the beginning of the paper. This, however, does not give the slightest reason to think that the questions—the first-person question and the question about life in general—are therefore not genuine questions. On the contrary, because they are genuine questions, and the questions that they are, they form part of the syndrome. If I speak of a 'syndrome' this is, partly, because I am thinking of cases where the trouble lies largely in the person himself. However, there is also the case where tragedy sometimes destroys the meaning that a person found in life. How does it come to make this difference? I have deliberately ignored the case of tragedy because this is not a question on which I feel competent to speak.

Why and in what sense are the questions we have been concerned with questions about meaning and intelligibility? What I said here was brief and incomplete. I suggested certain connections between the notions of the meaning of a word or sentence, the meaning of an utterance in a person's mouth (what he meant by those words, whether he meant them in this or that way), the meaning of an action, and the meaning that a person finds in what he does (what it means to him). There is a great deal here that needs investigation.

I have also hinted at a two-way commerce between certain preoccupations that are central to philosophy and the kind of preoccupation behind the words 'Is there meaning in life?', 'Is there meaning in my life?' I have suggested that in extremes the two questions, 'Can one understand anything?' as the philosophical sceptic asks this, and 'Is there any meaning in life?' as Tolstoy may have asked this question, meet. But here too there is a great deal of work that needs to be done.

Postscript

1. *Two questions contrasted.* 'Is there meaning in life?' or 'Has life any meaning?' and 'Is there meaning in his life?' or 'Has his life any meaning?' I have suggested that these questions are by no means equivalent, although they are not unconnected. The first question is about life or 'the world', the second is about the person questioned. Yet although the person who asks this second question and the man whose life is under discussion do not stand in the same relation to that life, this question has a kind of 'objectivity' which the question about life or 'the world' lacks. If you ask me whether there is meaning in life or whether one can make sense of the world I can only speak for myself. In this respect this question is like many moral and religious questions: 'Is it shameful to be found wanting in courage in the face of danger?', 'Is it degrading for a woman to sell her love?', 'Is there a God?' Here it is entirely proper for one to speak in the first person, to prefix one's answers with 'I believe'. Whereas the words 'Is there meaning in his life?', at least on some occasions, put a question that

is in many ways like the question 'Is there love in his heart?' On reflection one may conclude that whatever anyone else may think of the way he lives one has to admit that it does really make sense to him.

One may affirm that there is meaning in life and yet admit that one has lost sight of it in one's own life. It may be, for instance, that given the conditions in which a person is constrained to live, he is unable to make sense of his life, although he does not think that those who find life meaningful are deluded—even those who may be constrained to live under the same conditions. He may, in all his dejection, sincerely think that he can learn from them. Or one may deny that there is meaning in life:

> Among the coral crypts beneath the sea,
> Festoons of fishes weave insanity.[1]

Here it need not be that one finds life empty or feels it to be 'gliding away from under one's feet', as Ivan Ilych did. People who have spoken of the meaning-lessness of life, or of the unreality of life, have not always meant the same thing. There are a great variety of cases here. I have restricted myself to cases where the trouble lies in the person himself. As I said, in most tragedies it is not that way.

One may realize that one's life has been meaning-less, or one may come to see that the life of a person one knows well contains a meaning which had pre-viously escaped one. One may see this in one's own life in coming to a new perspective in which one finds new meaning. Or one may come to see that one has no real interest in what fills one's life, that one does not

---

[1] Alfred Kreymburg. These two lines were brought to my attention by Rush Rhees.

really care for the things one does, that one's relations are false. When in the latter kind of case one realizes that one's life is meaningless this is largely a matter of recognizing the presence or absence of patterns which one has missed in the welter of the detail that makes up one's life. It is much the same when another person's life is in question. Finding meaning in life, however, is not finding out that something is the case in this way. Although it undoubtedly involves a change in one's apprehension and so contains the possibility of error and illusion, one cannot ask of a man who says that he finds life meaningful whether he is right or wrong—unless this means: 'Do *you* find meaning in life?' If he has found meaning in life then he may have found a new hope, for instance, a hope which his previous perspective on life excluded. Seeking and reaching an assessment of one's life or that of another person is one thing, seeking and finding meaning in life is another. In the latter case 'finding' comes close to 'making'. Whether or not one finds meaning in life at least partly depends on what one makes or is able to make of one's life. Hence one cannot find meaning in life for another person; though one can recognize something he has overlooked, convey it to him and thus make him see something he had failed to see. One can only find meaning in life for oneself.

Supposing that one were able to help someone see what his life adds up to and in this way guide him i his apprehension of its meaning. This would not be helping him to find meaning in life. However, there are transitions from helping a person see that there is more sense in his life than he recognizes to helping him find meaning in life. Besides, the case where a person does not recognize that his life is meaningful has as its

limit the case where he *will* not let it have any meaning. Therefore, to help him recognize that there is
meaning in his life may come close to helping him
recognize that there can be meaning in his life—if only
he would change in certain ways, meet this or that
differently. And this is helping him to find meaning in
life.

One may ask: 'What gives meaning to his life?'
The answer may be 'His family life' or 'Love' or 'His
belief in God' or 'His work'. But often it will be
impossible to answer this question in this way—and
not because one lacks any knowledge relevant to it.

A man who suffers an 'arrest of life', such as Tolstoy
described in *A Confession*, may intelligibly ask what
the meaning of life is, but when no longer suffering
from such an arrest he cannot say 'The meaning of life
is so-and-so.' For what he has found is not something
that can be summed up and said to be an answer to
his question. When his life becomes meaningful, when
he finds meaning in life, his question disappears.
This does not mean that his question was not a genuine
question. We call many different things 'questions',
and they need not all have a common form or logic.
Here the parallel with philosophical questions would
take us *some* way towards understanding the peculiarity of the question 'What is the meaning of life?'
asked by someone who can see no meaning in life. If
one could speak of knowing or finding out an answer
to this question this would be something which shows
itself in how one lives rather than in what one says. It
would be something that appears in what one says on
countless occasions taken together rather than in any
one single answer. One who genuinely exclaims 'What
is the meaning of life?' may learn to find meaning in

c

life from another person, but not from any information that this person conveys to him, nor necessarily from anything he says about life. He learns from contact with a man of character—a contact that changes him. He learns from what this man's maturity, courage, humility, honesty, kindness is able to inspire in him. He learns too from contemplating what this man meets in his life. This is what knowing and learning are like here.

What the man who was asking 'What is the meaning of life?' found is not an answer to his question, but meaning in life. And he may have found this by coming to a moral perspective which was alien to his thinking. If we say that this moral perspective gave meaning to his life, we mean that it is in this perspective that he found meaning. The meaning and the perspective are internally related. That is why it would not make sense to ask how or why it gave meaning to his life. It is for similar reasons that Wittgenstein argued that there cannot be a theory of sense or of inference, of language or of logic. He would have said that we cannot *say* what language is or what it is to follow a rule. We can take and discuss examples in which what speaking or following a rule comes to will be *exhibited*. If we vary our examples we shall also see that they need not come to the same thing, that they may take different forms. He compared the relations of such forms to each other with those of games to each other.

We have seen that a person's life can fail to have meaning when he, himself, does not recognize this. Could the reverse be equally true? Can there be meaning in his life when he thinks otherwise? Isn't the fact that he thinks that his life doesn't make much sense indicative of something that has gone wrong there? These questions are not easy to answer. If one compares 'His life is meaningful, though he thinks otherwise' with 'He says that his life is meaningless but he does not think so' and 'He says that his life is meaningless but he does not really mean what he says', one will see that the occasions on which one says these things form a continuum. As one moves from one of these occasions to the other it becomes progressively more appropriate to say 'He *will* not acknowledge that there is meaning in his life'. From this it is a small step to 'He is bent on destroying any meaning that his life may have'. In this way we approach the kind of case where we might wish to say 'His life is meaningful though he thinks otherwise'. But as we do so we also necessarily approach the kind of case where it would be proper to say 'His life is no longer meaningful'. We see that to answer the above questions means investigating how far the words 'His life is meaningful, but he thinks otherwise' can take us before they become self-defeating. This is best done in terms of examples.

2. *Life and logic.* I want to say a few words about what Tolstoy saw in the peasants he wrote about with admiration, and the sense in which he thought one could learn from their lives.

Take the example of Ivan Ilych. Did he not learn something from Gerasim, the peasant lad? Tolstoy leaves us in no doubt that Gerasim made him see a possibility to which Ivan's way of living had kept his eyes shut, a possibility that was excluded by the way he lived. Ivan Ilych had been caught up in a way of life that excluded the possibility of care for and devotion to other people. By his example Gerasim

opened up for Ivan what was a new possibility and
made him realize what was wrong with his life. The
possibility in question is one that is *internally* related
to a certain way of living.

We have a similar example in the case of Father
Sergius, who finally learns from Pàshenka what he
has been seeking his whole life. Tolstoy puts this in
Father Sergius' mouth in the following words:

> So that is what my dream meant! Pàshenka is what I
> ought to have been but failed to be. I lived for men
> on the pretext of living for God, while she lives for
> God imagining that she lives for men . . . Yes, there
> is no God for the man who lives, as I did, for human
> praise. I will now seek Him!

'There is no God for the man who lives for human
praise.' One could say: 'There *cannot* be.' This is a
logical statement. What Father Sergius had failed to
recognize was that one can live for God in living for
men, and more strongly, that one cannot live for God
if one turns away from men. Such turning away can
take different forms. It may take the form of putting
oneself at the centre of one's thoughts and actions,
of living a life in which one seeks the esteem and
admiration of others, or even of oneself, praise and
glory, mental comfort and even moral perfection—all
of which could be described as 'worldly rewards'. This
was the case with Father Sergius. Or it may take the
form of living a life in which one gives one's heart to
an abstraction, say 'the good of mankind' to which
individual men take second place. Or, again, it may
take the form of living a life in which one subjugates
one's will to a 'collective will'. In none of these cases
would it be possible for a man to walk with God.

Thus, by her example, Pàshenka opened up a new possibility for Father Sergius. She made him realize that he had been misguided in his choice of a monastic life. This does not mean, of course, that anyone who chose to live a monastic life would be wrong or self deceived. But Father Sergius had been. He saw, thanks to Pàshenka, that it was possible, after all, to seek God without shunning men. He would probably not have seen this had he not genuinely sought to find God all his life—however misguidedly. He saw not only that he had shunned men because, having confused it with living for his pride, he had thought it incompatible with living for God, but also how much what he had called living for God, and so what he had practised, was living for men in the sense in which he had understood it. In other words, he had, as Tolstoy puts it, 'lived for men on the pretext of living for God'. It was this that had stood in his way all along.

What I want to emphasize is that what is in question is the idea of learning from someone's life and example, and that this has nothing to do with learning a skill or a trade as Professor Flew seemed to think in a paper entitled 'Tolstoy and the Meaning of Life' (*Ethics*, January 1963). I also want to emphasize that there is a two-way dependence between ways of living and conceptions of what is possible and what is not, what is real and what is not—more briefly, between life and logic. This is intimately connected with the notion of opening up a new possibility, the notion of a life from which we can learn something. Tolstoy thought that he could learn from the life of the peasants and he illustrated what can be learned from such lives in many of his stories. He showed in

The Death of Ivan Ilych its bearing on a search for meaning in life.

3. *Tolstoy's peasants.* Of course the reality of discourse on meaning in life presupposes such forms of living as are required by the very possibility of spiritual problems and moral and religious difficulties. As Professor Hepburn puts it: 'Were life *never* problematic, were people *never* subject to arrests of life, it is unlikely that we should ever have acquired the expressions we are discussing.'[1] However, the word 'unlikely' here is too weak and mistakenly suggests that the connection in question is a contingent one. I should say that were life never problematic, etc., it is inconceivable that we should have acquired the expressions in question, developed the concepts we are discussing.

Hepburn further asks whether it can be said of Tolstoy's peasants that they had meaningful lives when the kind of hurdles and arrests that Tolstoy wrote about did not come within their conceptions. His answer, I think, is 'No'. His point is that one cannot describe or characterize a man's life and actions in terms of concepts which he does not himself possess, concepts which are foreign to his thinking. While I certainly agree with this general point, I cannot agree with an implication which I perhaps mistakenly read into some of the things Hepburn says—namely, that it is essential that a man should have a certain amount of intellectual sophistication if his life is to be said to have meaning, if it is to be possible for his life to lose its meaning. Intellectual sophistication has nothing to do with it, and the life

[1] 'Questions about the Meaning of Life', *Religious Studies*, vol. I, p. 132.

in which Tolstoy's peasants were taking part certainly admitted spiritual depth. I mean, it admitted the possibilities which underlie the intelligibility of the kind of questioning with which we are concerned here.

4. *Philosophy and life*. Hepburn touches on the question of what philosophy has to offer a man who is trying to find meaning in life. He says: 'On the highly particularised problems of giving meaning to an individual life, philosophy may not have much to say: but it is certainly concerned with what seem to be general threats to meaningfulness arising out of the human situation as such.' In other words, it is concerned with whether, for instance, a man who thinks that the inevitability of death makes it impossible for human life to have any meaning is under an illusion.

Certainly philosophy is concerned with questions of this sort—questions about the relations between certain concepts and the ultimate conditions that justify their application, questions about whether what seems possible is really so and what seems impossible is really impossible. A study that guides a man's thoughts on such questions can *sometimes* remove what confines his understanding of what we use these concepts to say.

I think, however, that there are closer connections between reflection on whether or not any form of discourse, and in particular discourse on meaning in life, can have sense, and reflection on whether or not life or one's own life can have sense.

In the *Republic* Glaucon asked Socrates why moral considerations should matter. He did not think that they do not matter, but he wished Socrates to show him why they do, to give him reasons. He thought that it should be possible to do so. Reasons here should show, he thought, why moral considerations matter, they should convince anyone who did not have regard for moral considerations that he ought to, and provide a rational basis for that regard in those who have it. The idea is that if one does not have reasons one would be acting irrationally in paying attention to moral considerations.

Thus Glaucon hoped that Socrates would be able to provide him with a philosophical guarantee, an ultimate justification of moral behaviour. In so far as he did not doubt that his request could be met, however, he was not a sceptic. Yet like a true philosophical sceptic, he could have become doubtful of this while still holding the belief that moral considerations matter. He might then have said that this is a belief that rests on faith and that it is a scandal to philosophy that it should be accepted without reason—a scandal because, if they cannot be justified, our beliefs in justice, decency, honesty and courage are no more than mere prejudices instilled in us by education. Hence the craving for justification. The misunderstandings behind such a craving run into other forms of philosophical scepticism.

The philosophical sceptic doubts that regard for moral considerations can be justified; he doubts that there can be any justification for moral behaviour. But a man may also come to doubt the importance of moral considerations; his moral beliefs may begin to lose their hold on him so that he finds it more and more difficult to see any sense in a life in which regard for moral values is active. His case is different from that of the merely philosophical sceptic, although there are transitions from the one case to the other. The man who is losing his moral convictions may ask whether it

matters if he does the things which previously he regarded as impermissible and unthinkable. He may
even wonder whether it matters what he does; he may
no longer be able to make sense of life. But the
philosophical sceptic has not himself lost a sense of the
difference between following the path of justice and
decency and departing from it. Like Glaucon, he may
want to know what that difference comes to and
whether in it one can find any binding reason for
living a life of justice. Unlike the man who suffers an
arrest of life his problem is a philosophical one, not a
spiritual problem.

One similarity between them is that both are thinking from outside the perspective in which one has
moral reasons for doing one thing rather than another.
What the philosophical sceptic has to understand is
that any instance of moral reasoning and deliberation
is carried against a background of norms and values
that are taken for granted. It is not they that are being reasoned about. On the contrary, if people did not
have regard for and adhere to such values as justice,
honesty, charity, humility, if they did not have any
moral convictions, they could not engage in moral
reasoning at all, situations could not even present
them with moral questions from the reality of which
such reasoning and reflection take their start. He has
to see that the very *possibility* of moral judgment,
criticism, reasoning and decision presupposes that
there are certain things that are not open to judgment,
criticism, reasoning and decision—though these need
not be, and in fact are not, the same for everyone.
This is not anything peculiar to moral judgments and
reasoning. Just as the request for reasons why one
should pay attention or attach weight to moral

considerations at least partly comes from confusion, equally it makes no sense to justify induction, to prove the validity of mathematics, to demonstrate the existence of the material world. In the case of moral judgments and decisions any reason that one may give for the beliefs in terms of which the judgments and decisions are reached would turn moral considerations into considerations of prudence or expediency. There is no short cut to seeing this; much philosophical spade work is needed before the philosophical sceptic can appreciate it.

The philosophical sceptic has not lost his regard for moral considerations. The source of his trouble lies elsewhere. It is his grasp of such notions as justification, proof, reason, evidence, doubt, guarantee and inquiry that is at fault, particularly as these are used in moral discourse, and also his appreciation of the role which moral (and also religious) beliefs play in a man's life as well as in the life and culture of a society. It is this that is throwing his understanding of the logic of moral (and religious) discourse and reasoning out of focus. Whereas the man who can no longer make sense of things has lost his regard for the moral (and religious) ideals in terms of which he had sought and so far managed to bring things into focus.

Each is asking a question, 'Why should moral considerations matter?', 'Can there be any sense in life?', to which no answer can be given from where he stands. Philosophical reflection can so alter the philosophical sceptic's appreciation of the sorts of context in which we talk of 'reason', 'justification', 'proof', 'guarantee', and of the role which moral beliefs play in moral reflection, as well as in the life of the man who holds them, that the questions he asks no longer trouble him. One could say that the reflection and discussion which removes his inclination to insist on these questions 'answers' them. Such reflection and discussion certainly improves his understanding of what it means to have moral convictions, to make moral judgments, gives him a firmer grasp of the affinities and differences between moral reasoning and deliberation and other forms of reflection.

The man who has lost his regard for the values and ideals that gave sense to his life needs a different kind of reorientation. Certainly reflection and discussion has a role to play here. But the reorientation in question is not simply an intellectual one; it is a change in the person concerned. Hence it requires a different kind of inspiration. Philosophy may succeed in removing intellectual obstacles that stand in its way. Philosophical reflection on the nature of religious belief, for instance, may free a man's thought from misconceptions about the nature of religious beliefs and so help the growth of the kind of understanding he can have within their framework. But it cannot provide the impetus to such growth. There is a gap here between the recognition of possibilities and commitment, and philosophy cannot bridge that gap on its own.

5. *Life and death.* I have mentioned the question of whether life can have any meaning when death is inevitable. It would be an over simplification to think that 'death is irrelevant', since the thought of death can lead people to think that it does not matter what they do. Yet it is equally true that people who are lucid about the inevitability of death can live meaningful lives.

What is relevant to the question we are discussing is

what conception one takes of death and so how one faces the fact that death is for everyone without exception. It is true that some people ignore its existence though they know, of course, that they will die. Just as some people behave as if they did not recognize the existence of other human beings as independent, autonomous individuals, some people live as if they did not acknowledge the reality of death, as if they thought their life was endless and the gifts they enjoyed not subject to decay. Some others, on the other hand, while not ignoring any of this, are nevertheless not able to accept it, to come to terms with it in their own life. They are so obsessed by the idea of death that it desiccates life of all sense for them. Their attitude to death excludes their being able to find meaning in life, their being able to live a meaningful life. If life is to have any meaning for them what is required is not that death should not exist, but that they should find a different conception of death, that they should face death in a different way. This is precisely what they find impossible when their main concern is with themselves, so that the sense of their life is dependent on the continuity of their personal welfare. They cannot find meaning in life because they are unable to come to terms with their personal annihilation.

Of course, coming to terms with death is not only coming to terms with one's own personal annihilation, but also with the loss of those one loves. Certainly the death of loved ones may leave a man so bereaved, so jolt him out of joint, that it leaves him without any desire to go on living. None of his previous activities, nor any other he can think of, will hold anything for him now, he will no longer be able to see anything in them to want to carry on. Once more if he is to find meaning in life what is called for is a new conception of and perspective on life and death, one in which his loss becomes tolerable and it becomes possible for him to develop concern for things.

Let me note in passing that those who find the idea of death tolerable because they come to believe in the immortality of the soul and thus manage to keep a sense of proportion and live meaningful lives, despite the once shattering recognition of the inevitability of death, need by no means be deluded. For a belief in the immortality of the soul need not be one that makes the existence of death in any way unreal. It is compatible with everything which they once found shattering, and need not be a way of finding serenity at the expense of lucidity—if that were possible. Belief in the immortality of the soul is not a factual or inductive belief; it is not a belief in an endless existence.

6. *Life and language.* How close is the sense of 'meaning' used in connection with human life to the sense of this word used in connection with human discourse?

In a piece of discourse or conversation there is a two-way dependence between the way the various things said bear on one another and their relation to the reality that is being spoken about—in other words between inference and sense. It is true, of course, that 'life is not a statement'. Still, just as the statements we make are governed by our relation to reality so is the life we live governed by our relation to reality. Without this relation both would lose their intelligibility. Think here of the life of a man who is said to have lost his reason, understanding and contact with reality, and is removed to a mental home. I pointed out earlier that the possibility of a statement being governed by the speaker's relation to reality and that of his life being so governed belong together. Just as his talk can degenerate into meaningless chatter so can his actions and activities lose all sense. Where his words have become little more than meaningless chatter he will no longer have anything to say. Where he merely goes through the motions of what he does he is no longer in what he does. Neither his words nor his actions come from or express any conviction, and it makes little difference what he says or does. We have nothing to learn from his conversation or his life. Where this happens a man will no longer be able to relate himself to others; he loses his understanding of himself and of others.

It is true, of course, that a sentence has meaning independently of when and where and by whom it is spoken, whereas the meaning and intelligibility of a life is individual. In other words, one cannot understand a life in separation from the man whose life it is. If words have meaning in a person's mouth this is because they belong to a language which exists independently of what he wishes to do with its words. He could not speak at all if this were not so. We must not forget, however, that the sense and identity of a man's life is not independent of those forms of activity in which others take part as much as he. This is what I was thinking of when I said that a man's moral, intellectual and spiritual life is not even conceivable in the absence of the ways of living in which he participates—ways of living many of which could not have developed apart from language. Certainly one cannot understand a life apart from the person whose life it is. But the possibility of a life having or failing to have sense goes with the existence of what constitutes the life and culture of a community. This is just as independent of the meaning which an individual person's life may have as the language he speaks is independent of what he means on a particular occasion in conversation with another person.

There is a close parallel between the rules of logic that govern a man's talk and thought, and the norms or values that govern his life and behaviour, as well as in what is meant by 'govern' in the two connections. The relations of logic to thought and of morality to conduct; the sense in which regard for logic underlies the possibility of meaningful discourse and that in which regard for moral considerations, of one kind or another, underlies the possibility of a meaningful life. Thus if what I say has any sense, if it makes a difference what I say, I must recognize certain combinations of words as ruled out, certain transitions as impermissible. Similarly, if there is any sense for me in what I do there must be certain things that I regard as impermissible. What in particular situations I regard as permissible and what not is a matter of what values I adhere to; it is determined by my moral outlook on life.

CHAPTER 2

PHILOSOPHIZING AND READING A STORY

D. Z. Phillips

IT has been said, with good reason, that there is a difference between philosophical doubt and practical doubt. When this is said, it is a way of emphasizing the character of philosophical puzzles and their resolution. Philosophy shows us something about things we know already; what it gives us is not additional information but an understanding of what is there to be known. The person who doubts whether he sees a man or a pillar-box in the fog has his doubts resolved when more facts become apparent. His doubts lift with the fog. But the philosopher asks whether he can be sure of what he sees when he is actually confronting a man or a pillar-box. If his doubts were practical, the philosopher should be placed in the same category as the neurotic or the madman. What the philosopher is asking, however, is not whether he sees, but what it means to say that he sees. It is the logic, not the facts, of the situation which eludes him. Because of this, we are tempted to say that his philosophical conclusions about perception do not affect what he sees. Philosophers with radically different views about perception have no difficulty in identifying colours, seeing people or locating pillar-boxes when they wish to post a letter.

The distinction made in the above paragraph applies to other areas of philosophical inquiry. In moral philosophy, political philosophy or aesthetics, for example, the philosopher is not concerned with making moral, political or aesthetic judgments, but with giving an account of what it means to make such judgments. Nevertheless, one cannot conclude that the philosopher's conclusions on these matters do not affect what he appreciates about moral, political or aesthetic matters. Although the point of philosophizing is not to have such an effect, it is undeniable that the method and conclusions of one's philosophizing often place limits on what can be understood about the mode of human discourse one is investigating. Of course, philosophical reflection may enlighten as well as obscure. We may become aware of a greater range of possibilities. In the present chapter, however, I want to show how it is possible for philosophical reflections in related fields, namely, in ethics and the philosophy of mind, to have a limiting effect in quite a different context, namely, in reading a story. The story I want to consider in some detail is Tolstoy's *The Death of Ivan Ilych*.

I *Philosophical Presuppositions*

The following argument may form the philosophical presuppositions which someone brings to the reading of a story. Sometimes it seems to us that there is not a great deal of meaning in another person's life, although the person himself does not seem to recognize this. Or we may say that a person who lives for certain things is deceiving himself. But, it might be said, we must be very careful when we speak in this

D

way. Because of arrogance and shortsightedness, we may feel that our way of life is so important and so satisfying, that we cannot see what others could possibly see in other ways of life. Shortsightedness or ignorance about the kind of people we are judging may lead us to say that they put little into their lives and get little out of them. But if we saw the people we judge as they are, and not as we had taken them to be or thought they ought to be, we might have to revise our judgments. If we paid the kind of attention to their lives that we pay to our own, we would be led to recognize a variety in people's conceptions of what is important in life.

Because of these arguments we may conclude that whether a person's life is meaningless, or whether a person is deceiving himself, must be demonstrable in terms of what that person himself says, thinks and does. His life may be very different from our own. But although we could hardly imagine ourselves living in that way, all we can say is that such a life would be meaningless to us, not that his life is meaningless. Yet, if we reach these conclusions, how can we account for the fact that people do say that the lives of other people are meaningless when those people do not realize this, or for the fact that someone may say that an earlier period in his own life was meaningless even when he did not recognize this? These judgments seem to be ruled out if we say that it is what a person himself says or thinks which is the sole criterion of whether his life has meaning. On the other hand, we do not want to say that as long as a person says his life is meaningful it follows that it is meaningful. How, then, are these difficulties to be resolved?

Dr İlham Dilman has argued in Chapter 1 that however these difficulties are resolved, the criteria of whether a person's life is meaningless must somehow or other be the criteria of the person whose life we are talking about. If we say that someone has not recognized that his life is meaningless, we do not reach this conclusion by applying to his life our own personal standards. Dilman argues that it does not follow 'that there are not perfectly good standards for us to appeal to in judging another person's life. There are—namely, those of the other person' (p. 3). Dilman says that 'The only way to discover these is to study the person and the way he lives. But though they are personal, this does not mean that they are not objective in the sense that other people can use them as well as he. They can. It is because others can use them that it is possible for another person to point out to him what he has failed to recognize. If this were not so we could not distinguish between appearance and reality here. My point is that we do' (pp. 3–4). What are Dilman's general conclusions? He wants to say that if a person's life is genuinely meaningful to him, then it is, no matter what we think about it. 'If, on the other hand, one suspects that it is not a meaningful life then', Dilman argues, 'whether one's suspicions are well founded or not, what one is suspecting is that it does not really mean very much to the person whose life it is whether he recognizes this himself or not. If this is the case, both his life and his personality will bear marks of it' (p. 4). On this view, if we say that a person's life has little meaning, what we are suspecting is that it does not really mean much to the person himself, whether he recognizes this himself or not. If this is the case, the person's life and personality will bear marks of it.

It must be clear that Dilman's analysis is not confused in itself. On the contrary, it may be a perfectly correct and illuminating account of many cases where we do say that a person's life is meaningless. But it is presented as more than that. It is presented as the condition of the possibility of saying that a person's life is meaningless when he himself does not recognize this; this is what is necessarily involved in making such judgments. What we have here, therefore, is a theory about judgments concerning the meaning of life, a set of philosophical presuppositions. Whenever someone in the grip of these presuppositions discovers a situation in which someone says another person's life is meaningless, though he does not recognize it, or when he hears someone say that an earlier period of his life was meaningless though he did not recognize it, he will analyse the situations in terms of Dilman's theory. I want to show how a situation of this kind is found in Tolstoy's story, *The Death of Ivan Ilych*, and how Dilman's philosophical presuppositions determine his reading of the story.

II *The Consequences for a Story*

In *The Death of Ivan Ilych* a man on his death-bed looks back over the life he has led, and judges it to have been meaningless. As that life is unfolded in the story, the reader too may concur with Ivan Ilych's judgment. Dilman says that Tolstoy's story 'gives a very profound portrait of a man whose life has been meaningless though he has failed to recognize this himself. It shows us what the recognition of this comes to' (p. 19). The story concerns a man whose life in the context of government legal appointments has been one of steady but reliable progress. Suddenly, through an accident which brings on an illness which is to prove fatal, all this is brought to an end. Confined to his bed he is given an opportunity to reflect on the life he has lived. Despite his attempts to avoid it, he comes to see that the life he has lived has been meaningless. The question Dilman is interested in is what this recognition involves.

If Ivan Ilych says *now* that his life has been meaningless, then, according to Dilman, his life could not have had much meaning for him even during the period when he did not recognize this. But in order to establish this, Dilman has to locate features of Ivan's life during the period in question to vindicate his analysis. He attempts to do so by referring to three features which he takes to be characteristic of Ivan's life. It is not really his life, Dilman argues: that is, it is not the life he would have lived had he been true to himself. He speaks of the central needs and wishes of Ivan's life as having something fake about them, and says, 'What I meant was that he would not have needed to achieve a great deal of what he strived after if he had not wanted desperately to avoid facing the anguish and depression in his heart' (p. 19). We can see how the first characteristic of Ivan's life meets the requirements of Dilman's analysis. If Ivan says his life is meaningless it must be shown to be meaningless to him even at the time he does not recognize this. This is borne out, it is suggested, by seeing how the life he leads is a screen erected by Ivan to shield himself from the anguish and depression in his heart. The second characteristic of Ivan's life which Dilman mentions is its *negative character*, by which he means 'that a great deal of it is directed by the need to stave

off something—fear, guilt, depression' (p. 20).
Thirdly, Dilman mentions the *destructive character* of
Ivan's life, the failure to make operative that which
would avoid such destruction, his inability to love or
to care.

Notice that Dilman's judgment that Ivan's life is
meaningless seems to ignore the nature and content
of that life. What I mean is this: what makes Ivan's
life meaningless for Dilman is not the fact that Ivan
lived for the kinds of things he did live for, but the
fact that these things *are used to stave off something
else*. One might almost say that Dilman's basis for
saying that Ivan Ilych's life was meaningless is not
that way of life, but the use Ivan made of it, namely,
to stave off anguish and depression. But, surely, it
cannot be denied that someone could follow the same
way of life as Ivan Ilych *without that life being used in
the same way in which Dilman alleges Ivan Ilych used it*.
Couldn't a man live for the kind of things Ivan Ilych
lived for, not because he needed those things to stave
off anything else, but simply because those were the
things he wanted to live for? Clearly, it seems to me,
the negative qualities and alienation Dilman refers to
need not be present. As we have seen, according to the
analysis we are considering, if a man lives the kind of
life Ivan Ilych lived these characteristics *must* be
present. But what sort of 'must' is this? Is it not a
piece of philosophical legislation which falsifies the
facts and obscures possibilities? The only reason anyone would have for saying that these characteristics
must be present is that without them the prior philosophical analysis of what is involved in recognizing
that a life is meaningless is shown to be inadequate.
As we have seen, according to the proposed analysis,

such recognition involves locating some features of the person's life *prior* to the recognition which show that he too did not see a great deal of meaning in his life even then. Furthermore, it is suggested that when a person comes to see meaning in his life, what he comes to is something he has wanted all along. What we see happening here is a philosophical theory determining our reading of the facts. What should be the case is that the facts should determine what is shown in the philosophical analysis.

I have tried to show how a particular philosophical analysis of judgments concerning the meaning of life makes it necessary for Dilman to find certain characteristics in the life of Ivan Ilych. It remains to be shown that if we come to Tolstoy's story with these presuppositions, the likelihood is that we shall misrepresent and distort the kind of life Ivan Ilych led, and the kind of recognition he attained when he came to see that life as meaningless.

III *Waiting on the Story*

What sort of life did Ivan Ilych lead? Tolstoy gives an indication of the features of his life in the reactions of Ivan's relatives and colleagues to his death. As far as his colleagues were concerned, 'Besides considerations as to the possible transfers and promotions likely to result from Ivan Ilych's death, the mere fact of the death of a near acquaintance aroused, as usual, in all who heard of it the complacent feeling, that "it is he who is dead and not I" ' (p. 96).[1] Ivan shared these

[1] Leo Tolstoy: *The Death of Ivan Ilych and Other Stories*, trans. by Aylmer Maude, Signet Classic, The New American Library, 1960.

attitudes, attitudes which consist largely in expecting one's life to progress slowly but surely, the feeling that one has a right to expect things to go one way rather than another. Within such attitudes, there is no place for death. The end of the game is something which cannot be contemplated when the point of the game one is playing is the hope of unending progress. When Peter Ivanovich goes to sympathize with his colleague's widow, he meets another of his colleagues there who 'winked at him, as if to say: "Ivan Ilych has made a mess of things—not like you and me"' (p. 97). Ivan's widow's main interest is in finding out from Peter Ivanovich whether there is any way in which she can obtain a bigger widow's pension. These were the kind of interests which dominated Ivan. From his youth he assimilated the so-called liberal practices of people of high station. At school, he found that what he believed to be wrong was the done thing, so he managed not to remember that these practices were wrong. More conformity follows his passing through law-school and his first appointment. He has discreet affairs; the kind expected of youth. After certain legal reforms and the introduction of new judicial institutions, new men were needed, and Ivan became one of them. He is appointed an examining magistrate and so cordially terminates his old friendships. The chief attraction of his post was its power. He did not abuse this power. What was important to him was that he had it; things were within his control. He soon began to eliminate all aspects of his life other than those connected with his work. Ivan had married a brilliant woman with good family connections and a little property. The marriage did not interfere with his work. Indeed, it enhanced his reputation. Things change, however, when his wife becomes pregnant. 'He now realized that matrimony . . . was not always conducive to the pleasures and amenities of life, but on the contrary often infringed both comfort and propriety, and that he must therefore entrench himself against such infringements' (p. 110). Ivan's reaction to the attentions demanded by his wife illustrate how it is his way of life which determines for Ivan what is to count as relevant and what is to count as an infringement. Ivan thoroughly enjoys the dignity, pomp and power involved in his office. All this was as it should be for Ivan: his life 'continued to flow as he considered it should do—pleasantly and properly' (pp. 111–12). Ivan's life is not one of driving ambition, but it is one in which he expects a certain order, a steady progress of events.

Suddenly, Ivan finds that he has been passed over for promotion to a certain post. He is plunged into deep depression and all his relationships are soured by his disappointment. His irritation with his employers is obvious, and this leads to his being passed over for further appointments. Now according to Dilman, Ivan's way of life can be explained as a screen erected by him to hide from himself the anguish and depression in his heart. But the foregoing shows that the very reverse is true! We can only understand the character of Ivan's depression in terms of the life he is living. If we say with Dilman that it is Ilych's depression which explains his way of life, how do we explain his depression? That seems to remain an unresolved mystery. What needs to be recognized is that his anguish and depression *are the product, not the explanation*, of Ivan's life. They can be seen as the product of Ivan's egocentricity and desire for compensation.

By Ivan's egocentricity and desire for compensation I mean his tendency to see the importance of all issues as determined by their relation to himself, to think that he has a right to expect his life to go in one direction rather than another, to think that his fortunes and misfortunes are the only real fortunes and misfortunes, that his own life exhausts the meaning of reality. Ivan's egocentricity and need for compensation are illustrated by his reaction to his being passed over for promotion: 'Ivan Ilych felt himself abandoned by everyone' (p. 113). They are shown in the contrast between the way in which *he* regards the event, and the way it appears to other people: 'what was for him the greatest and most cruel injustice appeared to others a quite ordinary occurrence' (p. 112). Ultimately, however, the views of other people about his misfortune are unreal and irrelevant to him. Ivan Ilych thought that 'He alone knew . . . his position was far from normal' (p. 113). Normality, for Ivan Ilych, is understood in terms of his egocentricity and need for compensation: what is normal is that things should go well for him; what is not normal is that he should suffer any setbacks. Simone Weil has shown that this kind of egocentricity and need involves the illusion that the past has given us some rights over the future. What she says illustrates perfectly the kind of view of life Ivan Ilych possessed. She refers to the feeling that we have a right to a certain permanence: 'When we have enjoyed something for a long time, we think that it is ours, and that we are entitled to expect fate to let us go on enjoying it' (p. 173).[1] Ivan Ilych certainly feels that he has a

[1] Simone Weil: 'Concerning the "Our Father" ' in *Waiting On God*, trans. by Emma Craufurd, Fontana Books, 1959.

right to expect his life to continue along a course of steady progress. When that progress is halted by a setback, in Ivan Ilych's eyes, things are not what they *ought* to be. Ivan goes to Petersburg with the sole intention of getting a job with a salary of 5,000 roubles 'and be in a ministry other than that in which they had failed to appreciate him' (p. 113). His leaving, in his eyes, would be a punishment on the ministry. This is another instance of his egocentricity. Luckily, because of a shuffling of personnel he is promoted in his former ministry and is given a salary which places him two stages above his former colleagues. 'All his ill humour towards his former enemies and the whole department vanished, and Ivan Ilych was completely happy' (p. 114). But Ivan did not regard the change in his fortunes as a piece of luck, but as a restoration of normality, a return to the way things *should* be: 'after a stumble, his life was regaining its due and natural character of pleasant lightheartedness and decorum' (p. 114). His greatest pleasure was playing bridge: 'After a game of bridge, especially if he had won a little (to win a large sum was unpleasant), Ivan Ilych went to bed in specially good humour' (p. 119).

Ivan Ilych's life is not to resume its former course, however. While demonstrating to an upholsterer how he wanted the hangings draped in his new house, he slips on the step-ladder and knocks his side. He takes little notice of the matter at the time, but the pain in his side becomes more frequent and severe. He cannot get any satisfactory answer from his doctor regarding the severity of his illness. His wife's attitude is that the illness is his own fault, and that he will get over it if only he'll follow the doctor's instructions. For his wife, everything is a matter of planning. Of course, her attitude is but a reflection of Ivan's own. It is important to note that the first crack in Ivan's attitude is brought about by an *accident*, by a contingency, by something which cannot be planned. According to Dilman's account, the illness simply occasions the opportunity for reflection. What I am suggesting is that Tolstoy's depiction of how the illness occurred is meant to be a contrast to, and an indication of, the kind of attitude to life Ivan had prior to the illness. For Ivan, his illness is not part of how things should be. This is illustrated, in the early days of his illness, by his irritation at any little thing which was out of place, such as a stain on the table. Later, he is faced by the unavoidability of death. He does not know what to make of it. His only consolation is that everyone's turn will come. He cannot cope with the thought of his own death because up to this point he has thought only of other people's deaths as events in his life. He has treated their deaths as signs that they have messed things up; precisely the same attitude which Schwartz and Peter Ivanovich were to take of his death. But as his *own* death approaches, he sees that he cannot view it in that way. He sees that 'Death is not an event in life: we do not live to experience death' (6.4311).[1]

> The syllogism he had learnt from Kiezewetter's Logic: 'Caius is a man, men are mortal, therefore Caius is mortal' had always seemed to him correct as applied to Caius, but certainly not as applied to himself. That Caius—man in the abstract—was mortal, was perfectly correct, but he was not Caius, not

[1] Ludwig Wittgenstein: *Tractatus Logico-Philosophicus* trans. by D. F. Pears and B. F. McGuinness, Routledge & Kegan Paul, 1961.

an abstract man, but a creature quite, quite separate from all others. He had been little Vanya, with a mamma and a papa, with Mitya and Volodya, with the toys, a coachman and a nurse, afterwards with Katenka and with all the joys, griefs, and delights of childhood, boyhood and youth. What did Caius know of the smell of that striped leather ball Vanya had been so fond of? Had Caius kissed his mother's hand like that, and did the silk of her dress rustle so for Caius? Had he rioted like that at school when the pastry was bad? Had Caius been in love like that? Could Caius preside at a session as he did? 'Caius really was mortal, and it was right for him to die; but for me, little Vanya, Ivan Ilych, with all my thoughts and emotions, it's altogether a different matter. It cannot be that I ought to die. That would be too terrible'.

Such was his feeling.

'If I had to die like Caius I should have known it was so. An inner voice would have told me so, but there was nothing of the sort in me and I and all my friends felt that our case was quite different from that of Caius. And now here it is!' he said to himself. 'It can't be. It's impossible! But here it is. How is this? How is one to understand it?' (pp. 131–2)

Ivan's inability to cope is a direct result of the desire for permanence and control which I mentioned earlier. The view of life which involves such inability has been described penetratingly by Simone Weil.

Our personality is entirely dependent on external circumstances which have unlimited power to crush it. But we would rather die than admit this. From our point of view the equilibrium of the world is a combination of circumstances so ordered that our personality remains intact and seems to belong to us. All the circumstances of the past which have wounded our personality appear to us to be disturbances of balance which should infallibly be made up for one day or another by phenomena having a contrary effect. We live on the expectations of these compensations. The near approach of death is horrible chiefly because it forces the knowledge upon us that these compensations will never come. (p. 174)

When we come to consider Ivan Ilych's reaction to the recognition of the reality of death, there may seem much to commend Dilman's philosophical account of how Ivan's life prior to the recognition should be regarded. I shall try to show, however, that the passages which might be cited to support Dilman's analysis do not in fact support it, but rather, underline its inadequacies.

The first thing Ivan did, Tolstoy tells us, was to try 'to get back into the former current of thoughts that had once screened the thought of death from him' (p. 132). Tolstoy's way of expressing this fact may have misled Dilman. Dilman takes the above to mean that Ivan used his way of life to screen from himself the thought of death. What I am saying, for reasons I have elaborated, is that *it is the life he leads which screens the thought of death from Ivan*; because it was the kind of life it was it made it impossible for the participants in it to have anything but superficial attitudes towards death.

To try to save himself from his new-found sense of hopelessness 'Ivan Ilych looked for consolations—new screens' (p. 133). Again, this fact in no way supports Dilman's analysis. This search for screens is something Ivan indulges in *after* his recognition of the inevitability of death. It can only be understood in terms of his fear of death. One can in no way infer from this present activity the fact that Ivan's whole life in the past has been used as a screen by him. The search for consolations is an attempt to disguise the horror of death. But the search for screens fails: '*It* penetrated them and nothing could veil *It*' (p. 133). Ivan is tormented by the deception which grips everyone around him. No one will see his death for what it is. They keep treating it as a barrier to be surmounted. It is the lives they lead, the kind of life Ivan used to lead, which makes it impossible for them to entertain thoughts about the finality of death.

When Ivan says that he would like to live as he lived before, he suddenly realizes that this is not true. The things which mattered to him then now seem utterly empty. 'It is as if I had been going downhill while I imagined I was going up. And that is really what it was. I was going up in public opinion, but to the same extent life was ebbing away from me. And now it is all done and there is only death' (p. 148). Ivan is forced to recognize that he has not lived as he ought to live. Tolstoy's description of what this recognition involves may again seem to support Dilman's analysis: 'It occurred to him that what had appeared perfectly impossible before, namely that he had not spent his life as he should have done, might after all be true. It occurred to him that his scarcely perceptible attempts to struggle against what was considered good by the most highly placed people, those scarcely noticeable impulses which he had immediately suppressed, might have been the real thing, and all the rest false' (p. 152). This is the strongest evidence Dilman could appeal to in the story, but I do not think it yields his conclusions. The point is not that Ivan's life was a way of concealing these things from himself, or of shielding himself from them. On the contrary, he suppresses these things because they constitute threats at the time to what he really wants—the satisfaction of his need for compensation. What Ivan was brought to see during the night is *something new*, something which reflecting on death has revealed to him. 'In the morning when he saw first his footman, then his wife, then his daughter, and then the doctor, their every word and movement confirmed to him the awful truth that had been revealed to him during the night. In them he saw himself—all that for which he had lived—and saw clearly that it was not real at all, but a terrible and huge deception which had hidden both life and death' (p. 152). As a result of his reflections on death, Ivan passes an unconditional judgment on his former life and calls it meaningless.

Having made this judgment, however, Ivan still does not see how the past can be rectified. His present plight seems pointless. He cannot find any explanations: ' "There is no explanation! Agony, death. . . . What for?" ' (p. 151). What Ivan comes to see is that it is confused, though natural, to look for such explanations. He might have echoed Simone Weil's remark, 'If I thought that God sent me suffering by an act of his will and for my good, I should think that I was something, and I should miss the chief use of suffering which is to teach me that I am nothing. It is therefore essential to avoid all such thoughts, but it is necessary to love God through the suffering' (p. 101).[1]

[1] Simone Weil: *Gravity and Grace*, trans. by Emma Craufurd, Routledge & Kegan Paul, 1952.

The way in which something similar is to be revealed to Ivan has been hinted at by Tolstoy at different times in the story. At the outset, when we are shown the different reactions to Ivan's death, only Ivan's servant Gerasim is unafraid of death. When Peter Ivanovich says that Ivan's death is a sad affair, Gerasim replies, ' "It's God's will. We shall all come to it some day" ' (p. 103). Gerasim sees in death a truth for everyone, while Ivan and his colleagues saw at best a truth about Caius, man in the abstract, but one which certainly did not apply to themselves. Again, during Ivan's illness, when those around him will not recognize the possibility of his dying, Gerasim stands out as the exception: 'Gerasim alone did not lie; everything showed that he alone understood the facts of the case and did not consider it necessary to disguise them, but simply felt sorry for his emaciated and enfeebled master. Once when Ivan Ilych was sending him away he even said straight out: "We shall all of us die, so why should I grudge a little trouble?" ' (p. 138). Notice, Tolstoy puts what he regards as the true attitude towards death in the mouth of a servant, in the mouth of the man who serves, who cares for others. Understanding comes to Ivan Ilych too when he is able to care for others, when he ceases to be the centre of his world, when he is freed from his ego-centricity and need for compensation. It happens in this way just before his death:

> Just then his schoolboy son had crept softly in and gone up to the bedside. The dying man was still screaming desperately and waving his arms. His hand fell on the boy's head, and the boy caught it, pressed it to his lips, and began to cry.
> At that very moment Ivan Ilych fell through and

E

caught sight of the light, and it was revealed to him
that though his life had not been what it should have
been, this could still be rectified. He asked himself,
'What *is* the right thing?' and grew still, listening.
Then he felt that someone was kissing his hand. He
opened his eyes, looked at his son, and felt sorry for
him. His wife came up to him and he glanced at her.
She was gazing at him open-mouthed, with undried
tears on her nose and cheek and a despairing look on
her face. He felt sorry for her too.

'Yes, I am making them wretched,' he thought.
'They are sorry, but it will be better for them when I
die.' He wished to say this but had not the strength
to utter it. 'Besides, why speak? I must act,' he
thought. With a look at his wife he indicated his son
and said: 'Take him away . . . sorry for him . . . sorry
for you too . . .' He tried to add, 'forgive me,' but said
'forgo' and waved his hand, knowing that He whose
understanding mattered would understand.

And suddenly it grew clear to him that what had
been oppressing him and would not leave him was all
dropping away at once from two sides, from ten
sides, and from all sides. He was sorry for them, he
must act so as not to hurt them: release them and
free himself from these sufferings. 'How good and
how simple!' he thought (p. 155).

Ivan no longer thinks of himself. He no longer
wants to know why his life has gone this way rather
than any other. He sees the senselessness of such
questions:

'And the pain?' he asked himself. 'What has become
of it? Where are you, pain?'
He turned his attention to it.
'Yes, here it is. Well, what of it? Let the pain be.'
(p. 155)

Ivan is also able to say that death has been con-
quered. As long as he was in the grip of the need for
compensation, death dominated, since such an attitude
could not say anything in face of it. But Ivan over-
comes death in making something other than himself
the object of his energy and attention. To fear death,
for Ivan, is to fear the destruction of oneself, but since
caring for others for him involved dying to the self,
death itself lost its sting.

> 'It is finished!' said someone near him.
> He heard these words and repeated them in his soul.
> 'Death is finished,' he said to himself. 'It is no
> more!'
> He drew in a breath, stopped in the midst of a sigh,
> stretched out, and died (p. 156).

IV *Philosophical Consequences of Waiting on the Story*

I have taken a good deal of time over the discussion of
Tolstoy's story. There is no other way, I believe, of
grasping the nature of the understanding Ivan attained
on his death-bed. That understanding is obscured by
Dilman's philosophical presuppositions concerning
judgments about the meaning of life. According to
those presuppositions, if a man says that his life has
been meaningless, or if we make a similar judgment
about him, we must be able to show that during the
period of the life in question, his life did not really
mean much to the person concerned. By waiting on
Tolstoy's story we see that these assumptions can be
challenged as *general truths*. The story calls to our
attention one use of judgments about the meaning of
life in which they are unconditional judgments of
value. The life is condemned as meaningless simply

because of the kind of life it is. There is no suggestion
that before the judgment can be made by a person or
by someone about him, it must be possible to show
that the person himself did not really see much
meaning in his life even before he comes to recognize
it to be meaningless. None of the characteristics im-
plied by Dilman's philosophical theory need be
present. This is the case, I have tried to show, in
Tolstoy's *The Death of Ivan Ilych*.

I have said that moral judgments of meaninglessness are unconditional judgments: they do not wait
on what the unjust man wants or happens to think
worthwhile. *Despite* what he wants or thinks worthwhile, his life can be said to be meaningless. Moral
judgments intrude into, and constitute a veto on,
purposes however magnificent and means taken to
attain them however economic. J. L. Stocks expressed
the matter well when he said,

> The moral attitude is essentially a concern for the
> rightness of action. A true instinct exhibits it as
> interfering with the execution of purpose in stigmatis-
> ing as immoral the doctrine that the end justifies the
> means. The phrase implies that morality requires that
> all means shall be justified in some other way and by
> some other standard than their value for this or any
> end; that however magnificent is the prospect opened
> out by the proposed course of action, and however in-
> contestable the power of the means chosen to bring
> this prospect nearer, there is still always another
> question to be asked: not a question whether in
> achieving this you will not perhaps diminish your
> chances of achieving something still more important;
> but a question of another kind. 'There is a decency
> required', as Browning said; and this demand of

decency is prepared to sacrifice, in the given case, any purpose whatever.[1] (p. 77)

Ivan's realization of the meaninglessness of his life on his death-bed would not have the force it does were it not for the fact that it involves an unconditional judgment of value. Ivan does not deny that he had thought his life was meaningful. Now, however, he says that given the limits of that life, from a certain moral and religious perspective, it cannot be seen as other than meaningless. The philosophical theory and presuppositions we considered earlier do not allow for the possibility of such a judgment. This being so, the application of this theory and these presuppositions to situations where such judgments play a part is bound to distort these situations. This is true, as I have tried to show, of Tolstoy's story. Ivan, in the light of his reflections on death, sees his past life as meaningless simply because of the kind of life it was. Furthermore, when he comes to love and care for others, we need not conclude that this is something he has known or wanted all along. His remorse would not have revealed such a terrible pattern had he wanted it all along. What he has to face is that he had wanted other things all too much. What he comes to on his death-bed is something which dawns on him in the way I have tried to indicate. To think otherwise would be to rob Ivan's new understanding of the status Tolstoy ascribes to it—the status of a revelation.

[1] J. L. Stocks: *Morality and Purpose*, edited with an Introduction by D. Z. Phillips, Routledge & Kegan Paul, 1969.

CHAPTER 3

SELF DECEPTION

İlham Dilman

I

ONE question which both Phillips and I asked was:
Can a person's life lack meaning when he himself
thinks otherwise? In other words: Is it possible for a
person to deceive himself about his life? How is this
possible? How is it possible for him to deceive himself
about life? What is it we mean when we say that a man
is deceived about life? What is it we mean when we
say that he is deceived about himself? Or more
generally: What is it for a person to deceive himself?
In what I said in connection with these questions I
ignored the way in which a person's claim that he had
deceived himself or that someone else is deceiving
himself may involve value judgments. This is a
serious omission and, as Phillips has argued, it pre-
vented me from doing justice to what is portrayed by
Tolstoy in *The Death of Ivan Ilych*.

It is indeed true that we talk of self deception in
many different connections and that these do not
constitute any tidy category. Certainly there are
affinities that link them together, but it is not the
same affinities that run from one end of the spectrum
to the other. Consequently, it is impossible for me to
formulate anything like a theory or general account
of self deception. I shall, therefore, try to present a

few sketches or portraits of self deception which I find interesting, and discuss some of the difficulties which they raise for me.

I shall confine myself on the whole, though not completely, to instances of moral self deception; I mean the kind of self deception, for instance, into which people fall in their struggles to live a decent life, to make something of their lives, to find some sense or significance in life, or alternatively the deception they fall into in growing indifferent to moral considerations, in taking no notice of them. It seems to me that there is something important in the fact that people are prone to self deception in these ways. I find it difficult to imagine what moral and religious striving would be like if people were not prone to self deception.

I don't want to take up time with generalities now and so I turn to the first example that I wish to consider. It is an episode in Kitty Scherbatsky's life as portrayed by Tolstoy in his novel *Anna Karenina*. I want first, very briefly, to give the background to Kitty's moral and psychological problems, since these constitute the setting in which her self deception is to be understood.

Kitty is deeply unhappy. We are told that she is suffering from a broken heart and the humiliation of having been jilted. She and her mother, in whom she had always dutifully confided, had high expectations that Count Vronsky, who had been paying special attention to her, would before long ask her hand in marriage. On this account, she had turned down another suitor, Constantine Levin, whom she had known since she was a little girl, and for whom she had deep affection.

The situation comes to a head for her at a ball, after her having turned down Levin, when Vronsky ignores her and devotes all his attention to her sister-in-law Anna, in a manner, submissive and almost abject, which she had never known in him. After that night her health begins to fail, she loses her zest and interest in life, even her appetite. Her little world of happiness, in which everything was secure and well mapped and more or less predictable, collapses, her relation with her parents is altered, and she withdraws into herself. It is as if something needs to be worked out in her feelings, something which keeps her from contact with what was once the source of her joy in life.

For some time she remains in this state, then finally on the doctor's advice her parents take her abroad on a rest cure in Germany. There she makes friends with a girl named Varenka and a reawakening begins to take place in her. Varenka's life becomes a source of fascination and admiration to her, seeming to point to a way of working out what needs to be worked out in her soul. This has a moral dimension. It is bound up with the remorse she feels for having hurt Levin, for having grown apart from her parents and for having doubted them. She feels she has been ungrateful and disloyal. As she puts it 'You cannot imagine what vile thoughts I have about everything.' 'I feel', she says, 'as though all the good in me has disappeared, leaving only the evil.'

She attempts to model her life on that of Varenka, to emulate her selflessness. She seeks the needy, associates with invalids, tries to put their interests before her own. This is in part a way of seeking a solution to her problems, of working at those problems, however fumblingly. I mean that she is looking for a way to make amends for and to repair the harm which she feels she has brought about, to make up for the injustice she has done to her parents in her feelings and thoughts. She is trying to find a new significance in life, trying to become worthy of her parents' love. However, she is also tempted to take the easy way out; she tries to evade the pain brought to her by the realization of what she has done. Her desire to pay for this evil, to seek the good, constantly gives way before her desire to be good so she could be at peace with herself. Thus in her attempts to emulate Varenka she also seeks to reassure herself, to think that her anxieties about herself (and also about her parents) are baseless, that things are not as bad as they seem to her. Tolstoy draws our attention to this double-edged character of her activities in the words: 'In Varenka she saw that it was only necessary to forget oneself and love others in order to be at peace, happy and good. And that was what Kitty longed to be.'

In so far as Kitty succeeds in reassuring herself, in denying the evil she has perceived in her own heart, she falls into self deception. Her wish to reassure herself, her concern to find peace of mind, her desire to appear better to people, to herself, to God, falsify her moral strivings and make her a prey to another form of self deception. But let us first consider the self deception she falls into in pretending that her qualms about herself are baseless.

In Germany, Kitty succeeded in making herself believe that she was a better person than she *thought* at the time she was. As I pointed out, she was distressed by her own reactions, feelings and thoughts, which put her relations with other people, especially with her parents, in a new light: 'Everything (she says) seems vile, odious, coarse to me, myself most of all.' While this was not an illusion, it blurred temporarily her apprehension of the love and kindness of which she was capable; she lost touch with the good that was in her. When, in Germany, she succeeded in thinking of herself as good and kind, she did not regain the apprehension and touch she had lost. That had to await a change in her which was to come later. In other words, her precarious belief that she was good and kind was no genuine conviction; it was something forced, something that had to be continually bolstered up. So she was deceiving herself in that she was turning away from what she felt to be vile and odious in her. Yet, for all this, her thought of being vile and odious remained untouched, and continued to drive her to these measures.

Kitty turned away from what was distressing her by immersing herself in the activities which filled Varenka's days—tending the sick, reading the Gospels to the dying, etc. I do not wish to suggest that in these activities Kitty was devoid of sincerity altogether. She was not. Nevertheless the attraction which Varenka's way of life exercised on Kitty did not come wholly from what she saw in it. It came partly from the rewards it held for her, in the form of attaining goodness in her person, getting rid of the burden of evil that weighed on her mind and conscience, and finding peace of mind. That is, what attracted her to Varenka's way of life was something to which that way of life was to be a means. She had ulterior reasons for wanting to become selfless and live like Varenka; she was not disinterested in the actions and activities in which she engaged.

Obviously she could not recognize this and continue to act as she was doing. So she disguised her motives from herself and the character of her actions. She did so by allowing herself to be carried away by what she was doing and by avoiding to reflect on it. In this way she tried to convince herself that her doubts about herself were baseless. She further tried to keep from herself the true identity of the means she used to this end.

I speak of self deception here because of a movement in her life, at the time, to turn away from what the break with Vronsky and the surrounding circumstances had stirred in her. Self deception here takes the form of a strategy of defence and denial. In this respect Kitty is at once both deceiver and deceived, she is both the agent and the victim of deception. She is the deceiver in that she has herself arranged the setting in which she appears what she wishes to be—good, kind, selfless, true to her parents and in one piece. She sustains that arrangement while she continues to think of herself as bad and unworthy. She is deceived in that she is taken in by the appearances—appearances which she has herself engineered.

She is taken in, she succeeds in thinking of herself as good; and yet she continues to think of herself as bad. Is this a contradiction? Only in appearance. What is my reason for saying that she continues to think of herself as bad? Her whole behaviour. It is as if she continually needed to convince herself that this is not so. She would not need to do so if she were genuinely convinced. We can see, as she herself later realizes, that without the need to reassure herself that she is not as bad as she thinks, she would be freer to seek a better life, freer to seek it in the right way. She is not convinced that she is not bad: if she were she would

not need to go to such lengths—for in contrast with
Varenka she does not really have a calling or vocation;
she is not really a sister-of-mercy, as she soon realizes
herself. This is the gist of my reason for saying that she
does not think she is good, that she is not convinced.

But I also said that she thinks it, that she does
succeed in convincing herself that she is not bad.
Otherwise there would be no deception. Look at
Tolstoy's words: 'She recalled Petrov's emaciated
figure in his brown coat. . . . She recalled her own
efforts in the early days to overcome the repugnance
she felt for him. . . . She recalled the timid, touching
way he gazed at her and the strange feeling of compassion and awkwardness, and later a consciousness
of her own goodness, which she had felt at it. How
nice it was all!' Here one should remember that it is
for the first time since she fell into a state of depression
that she is beginning to find interest in life. Part of
this success story at this point supports the view that
she has managed to convince herself that she is not
'vile, coarse and odious'—to some extent at least. Hence,
for instance, 'the consciousness of her own goodness'.

'She thinks it' and 'she doesn't think it' as such, one
might say, contradict one another—in the abstract.
That is, in abstraction from actual and possible situations in which these words may be used. But I have
suggested that the reasons which support the one and
those which support the other do not always exclude
each other. In the example in question, I have tried
to show that they don't. On the contrary, they knit
together one of the familiar faces of self deception.

Kitty had also deceived herself 'in supposing that
she could be what she wanted to be'—like Varenka,
selfless. Here intertwined with self deception is a

genuine mistake on Kitty's part. As I said, her attempts to imitate Varenka were not wholly devoid of sincerity. She was truly attracted to Varenka's way of life. But in her zeal she underestimated the difficulties involved in self renunciation. The glamour that dazzled her in Varenka's way of life had clouded her apprehension and blinded her to the many dreary and tedious details that form part of it. Even the sacrifices that it would entail had seemed glamorous from afar. Besides she also had no clear idea of her own limitations. If this were all, it could be said that Kitty had made a mistake about the way of life that attracted her, and also about what she wanted and about herself. However, she had mixed motives and the glamour of a life of renunciation lay partly in the reward it held for her. This gave her a motive not to face up to her limitations, so that her not having a clear idea of them could not be attributed wholly to her naïve enthusiasm. When, in fact, she began to come to terms with her problems, and the pressure to prove her doubts baseless decreased, she was able to come to a more realistic assessment of the demands of a life of renunciation and of her own limitations in meeting them: 'She felt (as Tolstoy puts it) all the difficulty of maintaining herself on the pinnacle to which she had wished to rise.' 'She (also) became aware of all the dreariness of the world of sorrow, of sick and dying people, in which she had been living.'

I said a little earlier that her mixed motives in connection with the appeal of Varenka's life, her ulterior motives in her friendship with the Petrov family, the concern for rewards that was behind her kind deeds, lay Kitty open to another form of self deception. Here the deception is independent of whether or not she recognizes her ulterior motives and the true character of her actions. For we are no longer concerned with her deception about her motives, feelings, actions, desires, capacities and limitations. Kitty was not only deceived about her actions and re-actions, misconstruing their character and her motives for engaging in the various activities of which they formed a part. She was also deceived *in* them, deceived about what is important, about what counts in life. Her ulterior motives, her concern for rewards, *falsified* the concern she showed for the Petrov family and her kind deeds. 'It was all sham (she says herself a little later), it did not come from my heart.' What does not come from the heart here is meant to be the outcome of a calculation of gain. Her object (in her own words) had been 'to appear better to people, to myself, to God'. But why should that make her a prey to self deception *irrespective* of whether she is taken in or not? How is the falsity of her concerns, the impurity of her actions, connected with deception?

The notion of self deception brings in not only such ideas as being under an illusion, delusion or misapprehension, being blind, mistaken or misled, but also such ideas as acting, lying, pretending, being false, humbug and unreal. Now one cannot understand the notions of lying, being untruthful and being false simply in terms of either saying something false or conveying a false idea. I am thinking in particular of the contrast between *truth* and *truthfulness*, and their opposites. As Stepan Verkhovensky puts it in *The Devils*: 'All my life I've been lying. Even when I spoke the truth. I never spoke for the sake of the truth, but for my own sake.' Thus if, for instance, I open my heart to someone in order to show off or gain his approbation or sympathy (as Mme Hohlakov does in her confession to Father Zossima in *The Brothers Karamazov*) I cannot be said to have been truthful with him—at least not completely. What I am doing is not quite what it seems; there are strings attached to it. I have an ulterior motive, 'des arrières pensées'. There is something of myself that I am secretly keeping back, reserving. In the particular context in question, this is to abuse the other person's confidence. In some ways this is like not keeping one's word, or breaking one's promise. Here the other person is deceived not only in the sense that he is misled, but also let down. His trust has been betrayed, he has been led on under false pretences.

But how does this bear on self deception? Imagine someone doing his friend a good turn, pretending he does not care for what he, himself, gets out of doing so. So far this person has not deceived himself; he will not have done so until he is taken in, until he believes he is disinterested. From one point of view this is perfectly true and fits in well with the form of self deception we have considered. Thus the man who pretends to be disinterested, though he knows well enough this is not the truth, is to be contrasted with one who is taken in. The latter is self deceived in that he believes he is disinterested when it is obvious to others that he is not. This need not, of course, be obvious. Further, he is unwilling to recognize this, finding such recognition most unwelcome, and he is very likely the author of the belief, in the sense that he is engaged in make-believe. In contrast the former man is not self deceived.

Yet is this the only contrast possible, and from another point of view is not such a man self deceived?

Kierkegaard would have said he was. Why? Because
in his cynicism he is sullying and degrading himself,
betraying 'his own better self'. Such a man is using the
other person for his own ends. He pretends to act
selflessly while he never really cares about his friend—
and there is something terrible about eliciting someone's gratitude on false pretences. One could say, and
both Tolstoy and Kierkegaard would have agreed,
that in *using* human beings one is shutting one's eyes
to something that is in them and, ultimately, to something that is in one. Here one is deceiving oneself in
thinking that it doesn't matter. One is deceived about
what matters. So the claim that such a person is
deceiving himself involves the moral judgment that it
does matter. Therefore one cannot understand what
self deception comes to in this connection in morally
neutral, purely psychological terms. To speak here, as
Kierkegaard would, of 'being untrue to oneself', of 'disloyalty to one's own self or the denial of one's better
self', is to express a judgment of value. I shall say
more about this a little later.

For the moment I simply want to point out that if
one speaks of *double-mindedness* in connection with
Kitty, one would be thinking of the way she com-
promised and betrayed the very ideals she was striving to approach in her own life. In the very actions in
which she strived to approach these she betrayed 'her
better self', bartering what was most important for an
immediate sense of security, for an immediate relief
from what was weighing on her mind and conscience.
She was double-minded because her regard for those
ideals was tainted with her regard for rewards, so
that her very attempts to approach these increased
her distance from them. In Kierkegaard's words, she was

herself the obstacle that kept her from getting her
desire fulfilled, kept her from realizing in her own life
what she admired in Varenka's. For one cannot
succeed in becoming selfless so long as one seeks to do
so for the sake of the self—I mean, for one's own sake.
And this is what Kitty was trying to do. The fact that
she had an eye on what she could get out of emulating
Varenka's life continually cancelled her best efforts.

We see that there is a sense of self deception in which
to claim that a person is deceiving himself is to pass a
moral judgment on him. That is why I spoke of Kitty
as being deceived about what matters. In admitting
that she was deceived she would be accepting a value
judgment, namely that peace of mind and security, the
esteem and admiration of others, and even one's own
moral perfection, are not as important as she thought,
that there are more important things in life. She could
have said: 'I was deceiving myself in attaching importance to these things.' To say this sincerely is to
become a different person. Thus Tolstoy says that
Kitty had learned something from her experiences in
Germany. She had never been either immoral or
morally indifferent before. But now she became a
deeper person; her regard for the values she had
acquired as a child—kindness, love, charity, humility
—became deeper. This depth is inseparable from her
sense of the difficulty of realizing these values and of
remaining true to them. Kitty had also genuinely
been able to reconcile what in her feelings made her
vacillate between uncritical trust, naïve idealization,
and undiscriminating doubt. ('Papa began saying
something to me just now . . . and it seems to me he is
thinking that all I need is to get married. Mamma takes
me to a ball: and I think she is only taking me there

F

to marry me off as quickly as possible and to be free
of me. I know it is not true, but I cannot get rid of
these ideas.') Thus she succeeded in attaining a peace
of mind very different from the one she had lost—'she
was not so carefree and light hearted as before': her
world was no longer one in which evil is unthinkable,
and she had her own part to play in it for better or
for worse. This learning, then, which is the antithesis
of self deception, is a change in Kitty from light
heartedness to seriousness, from naïvety to maturity.

We have seen that Kitty's self deception did not
only have her actions, motives and feelings as its
object; she was also *morally* deceived. Here the
measure of reality implicit in talk of falsity and deception is a moral one. Yet the regard which the person
deceived has for the values which give us that measure
is *corrupt*. This is precisely what constitutes the form of
self deception which Kierkegaard called 'double-
mindedness'. Thus in the case of Kitty although there
is admiration for Varenka and a desire to emulate the
kind of life she lives, that admiration is not pure, the
desire not disinterested, not untinged with a concern
for peace of mind and self esteem. It is this that constitutes her moral self deception.

We have a similar situation in the case of Father
Sergius in Tolstoy's story by that name. Here is the
story of a man who devoted almost the whole of his
life to searching for God, for selflessness and true
humility. What originally sets him on this road is
finding out that the woman he loves and is going to
marry has been a mistress of the Czar he admires and
has pledged his loyalty to. This discovery changes the
whole course of his life, but not until much later the
spirit behind it. He has to go through many fires be-

fore that can change. The story illustrates how the very desires that initially turned him from army life to religion make it impossible for him to find what he seeks: 'Yes (he says towards the end of the story) there is no God for the man who lives, as I did, for human praise.' He had indeed tried to avoid worldly praise, but had done so out of vanity. This falsified his relation to God; it made what he practised sham. Obviously his soul did not remain untouched. As Tolstoy puts it: 'Sergius felt his own inner life wasting away and being replaced by external life.'

In the case of both Kitty and Father Sergius, then, we have an imperfect relation to certain moral and religious ideals, and a struggle to come to a better relation with them—a struggle against the inevitable evasion that comes from a concern for themselves. This concern thwarts and corrupts their moral and religious strivings by making their moral deeds and religious activities subservient to their own interest. Kitty and Father Sergius are, therefore, to be contrasted with the man who is or has become morally indifferent—one kind of example of which is again provided by Tolstoy in his character of Ivan Ilych. If the thought of good and bad were to come into the latter's actions and decisions this would not be the expression of *his own* convictions. He would be acting in bondage or servility to the opinions of what Plato called 'the great beast'. For the moral beliefs behind a man's judgments and decisions must be *his* if those judgments are not to be merely second-hand opinions, if he is to be doing more than merely the done thing. The case of the man who has *no* moral regard is the limiting case of the man whose regard has become corrupt.

Kitty, we have seen, was not solely motivated by the desire for relief and satisfaction; her search and struggles were not devoid of sincerity. Her life during her stay in Germany retains or regains youthful enthusiasm, a healthy desire to repair and make amends for the harm she has done, some degree of honesty, and a capacity for sacrifice and devotion, even though these are constantly corrupted under the pressure of her need for mental comfort. When she comes to recognize this, the way she betrayed the ideals exemplified in Varenka's life strikes her as something terrible: 'I'll be bad (she exclaims); but at any rate not a liar, or humbug.'

Father Sergius' case presents similar features. He had gone pretty far on the road to corruption before he found 'his childhood's faith which had never been destroyed in him'. The words are Tolstoy's, not mine.

> 'But after all was there not some share of sincere desire to serve God?' he asked himself, and the answer was: 'Yes, there was, but it was all soiled and overgrown by the desire for human praise.'

This desire to be the object of human praise had been strong in Sergius since his childhood and 'filled his life'. 'From early childhood (Tolstoy tells us) he tried in everything he took up to attain such success and perfection as would evoke praise and surprise.' This is something which Sergius brings to his new life, after he resigns his commission, to the detriment of what is to be achieved there. However, it is no less true that his religious struggles are largely struggles to purge his life of the desire to put himself in the centre. What had attracted him to religious life was the possibility (as Tolstoy tells us) of ascending 'a height from which he could look down on those he had formerly envied'. But this is only *part* of the story and, as again Tolstoy tells us, 'there was also something else—a sincere religious feeling which intertwined itself with the feeling of pride and the desire for pre-eminence, and guided him'. In his inaugural lecture on 'Moral Integrity' Professor Winch commented that these two are not distinct motives contingently intermingled, but that the latter is a corrupt form of the former. In other words, the religious feeling enters in Sergius' life by being implicit in his desire for religious pre-eminence.

While this is true and important, it leaves out, I think, something that is equally important. Winch would agree, I am sure, that the desire for pre-eminence, which mars Sergius' relationship with God, has an earlier history. This, however, is equally true of the religious feeling which is implicit in the form which Sergius' desire for pre-eminence takes after he becomes a monk. For that too has an earlier history; it existed long before Sergius could have sought religious pre-eminence. But even after he has joined the monastery it is not completely corrupted by Sergius' pride and his desire for pre-eminence. It does not exist solely in the form of a desire to achieve distinction in religious life. If it had, Sergius would have been a complacent monk, which certainly he is not. In what Tolstoy refers to as 'a sincere religious feeling' we have not only what keeps Sergius from resting in the corrupt form of his activities, but also what initially is in part responsible for the turn his life takes after he breaks off his engagement and leaves the Czar's army. For it was not only the possibility of distinguishing himself and outshining those whom he envied for their importance that had attracted him to religious life, but *also* the possibility of freeing himself from his pride and envy, of purifying his soul. It was this desire for purity which his sister Varvara had not recognized in him. Thus we have, after all, two distinct motives that are contingently intermingled—just as we do in the case of Kitty's attraction to Varenka's life. This seems to me to be typical of that form of self deception which Kierkegaard called double-mindedness. But double-mindedness is not the only form which moral self deception takes. Egocentricity is another.

II

A profound portrait of the latter form of self deception is given by Tolstoy in *The Death of Ivan Ilych*. Here, too, as in the case of Kitty, the moral deception is mixed with another kind of deception which can be understood in purely psychological terms. But I do not want to go into this matter now.

At the end of his life Ivan Ilych recognizes that his life has been empty and meaningless; he comes to see the vanity of everything he has lived for. As Tolstoy puts it: 'He saw clearly that all this was wrong: all this was a terrible, monstrous lie, concealing both life and death.' Part of what Tolstoy means by this is that Ivan had lived for the wrong things, and that they were wrong because the only kind of devotion possible to these things is one that excludes any real consideration of people. In this respect it is Tolstoy who condemns what Ivan had lived for. For Ivan to think that his life has been a lie is for him to come to Tolstoy's moral perspective. What his way of life had concealed from Ivan Ilych was in part a 'moral truth'.

Hence Tolstoy speaks of it as a lie and says that it had concealed from him 'life and death'. What it had concealed, in part, was the vulnerability of human beings and their dependence on each other, something in them that has a claim on our compassion, and also that the meaning of life cannot be found in oneself. Thus Ivan had turned away from what is important in life. This is Tolstoy's judgment of value; when Ivan comes to accept it he too sees his past life as a lie and deception. So he says: 'I thought I was climbing the mountain, while in reality I was going down it.' These words are preceded by the following description by Tolstoy of Ivan Ilych's reflections:

> In imagination he began to recall the best moments of his pleasant life. But strange to say none of these best moments of his pleasant life now seemed at all what they had then seemed—none of them except the first recollections of childhood. There, in childhood, there had been something really pleasant with which it would be possible to live if it could return. But the child who had experienced that happiness existed no longer, it was like a reminiscence of somebody else.
>
> As soon as the period began which had produced the present Ivan Ilych, all that had seemed joys now melted before his sight and turned into something trivial and often nasty.

Here then Ivan looks back on his past life and concludes that it had not been a happy life, whereas at the time it had struck him very differently. To see what is involved here let us contrast this case with another kind of case where a man looks back on his past and says that he had an unhappy life, though he also recalls distinctly, as also his friends do, that he had thought otherwise then.

This man looks back on his past life, considers his activities then, what he thought and felt, and all these now strike him differently from the way they struck him at the time. Then he would have said, and did say, 'I am perfectly contented with the life I live; I am happy.' Now he says, 'I was under an illusion; I was not happy.' And then and now the concept of happiness that enters these conflicting judgments is the same concept. What he is considering now and what he considered or was struck by then, is the same thing, the same period of his life, and his conception of what it is to be happy has not changed. But his apprehension then and now are different. Given the criteria of appearance and reality internal to this conception of happiness this man may have reason now to say or think that it *seemed* to him then that he was happy when *in reality* he was not. He would say, and we could agree, that he had been under an illusion, that he had been deceived. What is distinctive of this case is that the concept of happiness which enters his past judgment which is rejected as mistaken, or the past apprehension described as illusory, and the present one, is the same. In other words, the man's conception of happiness has not changed. One may put this by saying that the two judgments are made from the same perspective.

In Ivan Ilych's case this is otherwise. For here between the earlier judgment, 'I am happy', and the later one, 'I was not happy', referring to the same time of his life, there is a change of conception. From the one time to the other Ivan's conception of happiness has changed. Hence the conflict between Ivan's former judgment or apprehension and his present one cannot be as in the other case. For there the possi-

bility of the kind of conflict we have depends on the
conception operative at the different times remaining
unchanged. If there is a conflict in Ivan's case too,
despite the change of conception, this is because
implicit in his later judgment (as expressed in the
passage I quoted) is the claim that what he called
happiness is not to be called happiness, is not true
happiness, does not deserve to be called that—more
likely (as in the case of Antigone with regard to her
uncle's conception of happiness) it deserves to be
spat on. This is a judgment of absolute value. The
'true' in 'that is not true happiness' is a value term
and presupposes a moral perspective.

There are, then, two senses in which one may be
unhappy and not know it. In the one case one is blind
to one's feelings and reactions, one avoids recognizing
them for what they are—as in the case of the man who
is shocked or frightened but will not recognize it. In
the other case one's mind and heart are shut to a
moral perspective and so one fails to see one's life and
actions, one's feelings and reactions, from that perspective; one does not see them in that light.

When Ivan Ilych comes to see his life from Tolstoy's
perspective he says: 'According to public opinion (or
the view of the world, as Kierkegaard might have said)
I was climbing the mountain; and all the time my life
was gliding away from under my feet.' What shall it
profit you, as Socrates might have said to Thrasy-
machus, if by your cleverness and vigilance, you gain
the whole world, prestige, money, power, adulation,
and in the process lose your soul? This is what we
need to understand here, what it means to lose one's
soul, to become dead to any claims that what is good
and decent may have on one in particular situations,

to become callous and insensitive to other people. One needs to understand, what Tolstoy portrays so well, why and in what sense one is the loser here. This brings me to the idea of betraying one's better self which I mentioned earlier.

These ideas of 'betraying one's better self', 'disloyalty to one's true self', 'acting against one's real inclination', 'neglecting one's true interests', have their intelligibility in a particular context where one is prepared to make absolute judgments of values; just as the idea of 'betraying someone else's trust' (which I mentioned in connection with deception earlier) has sense only in connection with certain familiar moral concepts and in the kind of context where they are applicable. If, with Kierkegaard, we were to say of Ivan Ilych that he had continually done what he really would rather not do, these words would be reminiscent of the ones Alcibiades uses in the *Symposium* when he says of Socrates: 'He compels me to realize that I am still a mass of imperfections and yet persistently neglect my own true interests by engaging in public life. So against my real inclination I stop up my ears and take refuge in flight.'

The man in question, whether he is Ivan Ilych or Alcibiades, is represented as resisting some realization which would be a change in him. If he is said to be neglectful, or even evasive, he is moved by what has a strong grip on his will—ambition, the desire for success, in some cases a fear of insignificance. But in what sense is public life against his true interests? In what sense is he acting against his real inclination in pursuing a life of ambition? Earlier,[1] I thought that Alcibiades and also Ivan Ilych were not indifferent to what their

[1] See pp. 3, 15 f. above.

life excluded, that underneath, even if not in appearance, Ivan Ilych did care for the values he had betrayed. But this is a mistake.

The distinction in the *Symposium* between a man's
real inclinations and his apparent inclinations is not
the same as the one in terms of which we may be
thinking if we said of someone that although he continually neglects his wife, nevertheless he really cares
for her. Again when in *The Eternal Husband* Velchani-
nov realizes that 'Pavel Pavlovitch did want to kill him,
but the thought of the murder had never entered his
head', this is not the distinction with which Plato was
concerned. For the distinction between reality and illusion, truth and falsity, in terms of which Plato's Alcibiades and Socrates are thinking is a *moral* distinction.
Alcibiades' 'real inclination' is not something that is
necessarily active in his life, in however muffled and
muted a way, countering his ambitions and keeping his
conscience alive. In the words which Plato puts into his
mouth, Alcibiades is not commenting on some tendency
or trend in his life, there though not apparent. Rather
he is passing a judgment on that life, assessing its
worthlessness, the degradation involved in it, as seen
from Socrates' moral perspective. In the words 'my
real inclination' and 'my own true interests' he is expressing an awareness of what he *ought* to do, how he
ought to live, and not of what he wants to do or how
he would like to live. How he ought to live; a concern
for his soul—this is what he had neglected; not the
fulfilment of his desires.

It is much the same with 'one's true or better self'
used in this context. For it does not signify 'what one
is really like, underneath, when the chips are down'.
When one speaks of 'one's true self' here one is talking

about what one *ought* to be. What is in question is a
moral vocation. To fail in that, to betray one's true
or better self, is to fail morally, as an individual. The
identity between an individual person and his vocation, in this sense, is not one that is determined by
what he wants. It has a moral claim on his will regard-
less of what he wants. For although he is free to reject
it, that does not make him immune to a judgment of
condemnation. This is well brought out in an example
which Wittgenstein used to illustrate the difference
between an absolute and a relative use of expressions
of value.[1] In that example, the person to whom his
friend said, 'You're behaving like a beast', replied, 'I
know, but I don't want to behave better.' Unlike the
tennis player who had said that he knew he played
badly but did not want to play better, he invited the
retort: 'You *ought* to want to behave better.' In other
words, whether he cares to behave better or not he
cannot escape the judgment that he ought to. That is
why Kierkegaard speaks of the vocation with which the
better self is identified as 'eternal'. The point is that
one *cannot* opt out of it without inviting a moral
judgment on one's life; one *cannot* deny it without
suffering as an individual—whatever one may think
and feel. It is in this sense that Socrates' judgment in
the *Gorgias* on Archelaus' life is to be understood.

Of course, Ivan Ilych's life and character are very
different from those of Archelaus, the tyrant of Macedonia. For Ivan Ilych was a conformist, dependent on
routine and ritual. He was anxious to conform to
'what was considered good by the most highly placed
people': 'he considered his duty to be what was so

[1] Wittgenstein's Lecture on Ethics, *Philosophical Review*,
January 1965, pp. 5–6.

regarded by those in authority'. He was 'attracted to people of high station as a fly is drawn to the light, assimilating their ways and views of life'. These descriptions are Tolstoy's. Hence although his one concern was *himself*, the principles on which he acted were not his. There is nothing paradoxical in this. He was dependent on the values of the highly placed for the use he made of them, and his relation to them was obsequious, but he did not believe in them. Yet he was not contemptuous of them; he had himself to think of his actions as justified. He could be very ruthless, but always within the limits of this conformity. In other words, like Archelaus he had no regard for moral considerations and had made the various aspects and activities of his life subservient to his own ends. This is what I mean by egocentricity. But unlike him he was servile and at the mercy of other people's approval. It is this latter feature that contributes to the hollowness of his life. When Ivan realizes, as Tolstoy puts it, 'that his professional duties and the whole arrangement of his life and of his family, and all his social and official interests, might all have been false', when he says, 'all the time my life was gliding away from under my feet', to understand what he means we have to consider *both* these features—in other words, his egocentricity and hence his alienation from everything that may be said to be of the spirit on the one hand, and what contributes to the hollowness of his life on the other. With the latter I have not been and am not concerned now.

It is his egocentricity, his lack of regard for moral considerations, his alienation from the spiritual, that Tolstoy is thinking of when he says that Ivan Ilych's life had been a lie—'a terrible and monstrous lie', 'a

terrible and huge deception which had hidden both
life and death'. In other words, the things Ivan had
lived for, his greed, envy and self-centred ambitions
had excluded a moral perspective on life and death.
But the question, 'Why is that a deception?' cannot
be answered from the perspective of Ivan's egocentricity. One may be able to say a great deal about
what is involved in calling Ivan's conception of happiness false, in characterizing his life as a lie. But these
will not count as reasons for Ivan, justifying these
judgments and characterizations, until and unless he
accepts Tolstoy's perspective. All that one can do is
to contrast the perspective which Ivan Ilych reaches
at the end of the story with the egocentric outlook
that had dominated all his life, and try to show what
each involves and excludes. If one says that the perspective he came to at the end of his life is true, this
is the expression of one's commitment to it and for
this there can be no substantiation.

What I wish to emphasize is the *incommensurability*
between the life that is condemned here as a lie, a life
of deception, and the life from the perspective of
which this judgment is made. I mean that no considerations that one may put forward to Ivan, at the
height of his career, to show that he is deceived need
be counted by him as justifying what is said. This is
not the case with Kitty, as we have seen, nor, for the
most part, is it true of Father Sergius. There is an
important difference between Sergius' desire for pre-
eminence which corrupts his life as a monk, or Kitty's
desire for the kind of moral perfection for which she
admired Varenka, and Ivan Ilych's desire to be top
and the centre of the world.

D. Z. Phillips drew my attention to this point

once, in discussion, by contrasting *envy* and *admiration*. Kitty, for instance, admired Varenka whose life she wanted to emulate, whereas Ivan Ilych envied those to whose position he aspired. A person cannot be said to admire something unless he could be said to think of it as something good. This is not so with envy. It is sufficient for a person who envies someone on account of his position or possessions to think of these as things which the other person is pleased to have or enjoys having. In other words, admiration in a person, as opposed to envy, presupposes a recognition of certain standards. This recognition is essential to forms of ambition in which people wish and seek to become the object of such admiration without being prepared to live up to these standards. Hence a life in which such an ambition is operative would be a corrupt version of the life of a person who has a genuine regard for the standards in question and who puts them second to nothing. These two forms of life are therefore commensurable and the person living the corrupt form of life (like Kitty or Sergius) would recognize what is meant by saying that he is deceived. Sergius would have no difficulty in agreeing that *if* he were living for men, *if* he did not avoid prominence as a monk and hermit, or did so out of pride, he would be living a life of deception. He did condemn these things from within the life he led, and they revolted him when, for instance, he met them in the Abbot of the metropolitan monastery whom Tolstoy describes as 'a cunning worldly man who was making a career for himself in the Church'. Similarly for Kitty. When she recognizes her activities among the sick as being 'sham' she does not come to a new understanding of what is sham. That understanding is at least implicit in her life; her life does have a relation to the standards by which her activities abroad are judged as sham. Genuine regard for moral and religious ideals and its corrupt forms, which constitute self deception in the case of the double-minded, one could say, exist in the same logical space. Whereas when Ivan Ilych comes to see his former life as 'a terrible and monstrous lie' his whole geometry of life and death is transformed.

There is, then, no agreement over criteria of truth and deception, no common understanding, between one who says that the egocentric man is deceived and the egocentric man himself, between the once egocentric person and the new man who may be said to have risen in him after he has undergone the kind of transformation portrayed by Tolstoy at the end of *The Death of Ivan Ilych*. On the contrary, an enormous gulf separates them. If so, what more could 'He is deceived' or 'I was deceived' mean here than that I now *reject* a certain life, *reject* a particular conception of what counts in life and of what constitutes happiness. If one agrees with what I have said so far, one would be inclined to answer that it hardly comes to anything more than this, and that if the words 'I was deceived' or 'He is deceived' merely repeat the expression of one's moral beliefs perhaps it would be more honest to stop using them in this connection.

This, however, would be making light of that feature which the notion of deception, used in these connections, is meant to bring into focus. For what is characteristic of the life and outlook that I reject is the *enormous gulf* that separates it from the kind of life I have come to accept and the outlook I have acquired. Indeed, as Phillips put it to me in discussion, from where I now stand it strikes me as folly and madness.

It is precisely this that I am bringing into focus when I call the life that I reject a lie and deception.

What are the logical limits within which we can speak of deception in the sense now in question? Presumably we do not want to talk of deception or delusion in every case where a gulf separates us from the life, practices, understanding and outlook of other people. For instance, Wittgenstein invites us to imagine a people who pile timber in heaps of arbitrary, varying height, and then sell it at a price proportionate to the area covered by the piles. They even justify this with the words: 'Of course, if you buy more timber you must pay more' (*Remarks* I, paragraph 148). Here we no longer[1] know or understand what is going on—so much so that apparently Frege spoke here of 'a hitherto unknown kind of insanity'. But I would *not* want to say that these people are deceived or deluded. Perhaps there is not enough common ground *elsewhere* between us for me to want to speak like this. Another example would be the gulf that separates the Christian who believes in a Last Judgment and the man in whose life such an idea plays no part. Wittgenstein, who considers this example, points out that there is no common grammar or measure in which these two people may be said to hold opposite beliefs (*Lectures on Religious Belief*, p. 53). If either one said of the other that he is deceived or deluded I would understand why he spoke like this, but I would not want to speak like him.

The case of the egocentric man is different, however, in that no regard for any kind of moral consideration plays a part in his life. The relation of the

[1] As opposed to what we are invited to imagine in the previous section—paragraph 147.

positions of the egocentric man and men in whose lives regard for moral considerations play a part is *different* from that of the positions of men who have regard for different values, consider different kinds of things to be morally important in life, or from that of the positions of the Christian believer and the atheist. I should not want to say of any of them that they are deceiving themselves, as I would say this of the egocentric man.

The latter, as Gabriel Marcel put it, 'moves on the margin of reality like a sleep-walker' (*Homo Viator*, p. 22)—an image that comes from Plato. What one has to understand here is that the egocentric man and the worldly man remain insensible to a whole dimension of reality. Their life excludes the reality of everything that may be said to be of the spirit. Yet what may be called a life of the spirit admits of a variety of forms, by no means equivalent. There is a vast difference between the atheist or humanist to whom Christianity means little, although in his own way he lives a life in which spiritual values play an active part, and the man in whose life there is no place for *any* such values. Unless the use of the terms 'deception' and 'delusion', in the sense that is now in question, is confined to the latter kind of case, one could say of anyone with whom one disagreed morally that he was self deceived; anyone who attached importance to things in which one saw nothing would count as deluded for one. Clearly this would either trivialize the sense of the terms 'deception' and 'delusion', or it would be the expression of a kind of arrogance which would itself be a form of self deception.

To summarize. In this chapter I have been concerned with some forms of moral self deception. We

have seen that here talk of deception, illusion or delusion presupposes the reality of certain moral standards
or measures and has no sense apart from the universe
of discourse in which these standards operate. We
have also seen that the notion of a mistake or deception in connection with what is important in life is
very different from the notion of a mistake or deception in connection with matters of fact. A person may
be mistaken or deceived about his reactions and
motives, or about those of another person, without
being self deceived. The mistake may be an honest or
innocent one, he may be a passive recipient of the
deception. Whereas it would be difficult to imagine how
a person could be morally deceived without willing
the deception—though not necessarily *qua* deception.
Thus, as we have seen, Ivan Ilych and Father Sergius
were deceived in evading a moral truth, evading it in
the kind of life they lived. For a person to do so *is* to
neglect his soul or spiritual welfare. The self here is
the victim of deception in the double sense that it is
under an illusion, morally speaking, and touched by
evil and falsehood. Thus it is not only his vision
or apprehension that is affected, but his soul as
well—inevitably. The connection here is an internal
one.

A person cannot suffer this sort of corruption or degradation without entering into it. He *lives* the deception; he is moved by what has a strong grip on his
will. He is, therefore, necessarily also its agent. Thus in
moral deception a person cannot be a victim without
at the same time being an accomplice. Hence there is
no need to find any extra features in his life, in the
form of make-believe, dramatization, refusal to reflect, avoidance of certain situations, biasing of the

appreciation, and so on, to establish the complicity without which there would be no self deception. Whereas in kinds of self deception which do not involve judgments of value a man's complicity is a contingent fact; its relation to the deception he is under is an external one.

CHAPTER 4

THE DELUDED SELF

(A PHILOSOPHICAL DIALOGUE)

D. Z. Phillips

Callias: I should be grateful if we could discuss the following philosophical problem. Sometimes it seems to us that there is little that is worthwhile in another person's life. We seem to see something about his life which he himself does not see. But shouldn't we be extremely careful when we speak in this way? Such talk may be the product of arrogance or short-sightedness. Feeling his own way of life so important and satisfying a man may fail to appreciate what others see in other ways of life. Such lack of appreciation tells us more about the person who so reacts, than about the persons he reacts against. It is a symptom of his arrogance and moral blindness. Short-sightedness or ignorance about the kind of people we are judging may lead us to say that they put little into their lives and get little out of them. But if we saw the people we judge as they are, and not as we had taken them to be or thought they ought to be, we might have to revise our judgments. There is always a danger of imposing our conceptions of what is important and worthwhile on to the lives of other people. If, however, we paid the kind of attention to other people's lives that we pay to our own, we might be led to recognize a hitherto unrecognized variety in people's conceptions of what is important in life. Through giving this kind of attention we may become aware of a more extensive range of moral possibilities.

When I reflect in this way, I am tempted to draw the general conclusion that we can only assess whether a person's life is meaningful or worthwhile in terms of what that person says and thinks. What he thinks and says may not be the same as we think or say. Indeed, we may find it hard to imagine ourselves saying or thinking such things. Nevertheless, we cannot dismiss as meaningless the life in which such things are thought and said without regard to the person whose life it is. At most, what we should say is that such a life would be meaningless or worthless to us, or that we could never live in that way. But this is not to say, and neither would it follow from saying this, that the person's life is meaningless.

If I draw these conclusions, however, I am no longer able to account for the kind of judgment with which I began this discussion. Yet we do make such judgments, and we often make them with confidence. How can we say that a person's life is meaningless or worthless if he does not say this himself? How can a person say that the life he used to live was meaningless even when he did not recognize this? These things seem to be ruled out, since I have concluded that it is what a person says or thinks which is the sole criterion of whether a person's life has meaning. And yet I find that I do not want to say that as long as a person says his life is meaningful it follows that it is meaningful. If I did, I should be unable to allow the possibility of a person's life being meaningless without his recognizing it.

So you see, a paradoxical situation has arisen, and I cannot see any way out of it.

Semeias: I do not think that your conclusions do lead to a paradox. You are quite right in thinking that however your difficulties are resolved, the criteria of whether a person's life is meaningless or worthless must, somehow or other, be the criteria of the person whose life we are talking about. If we say that a person's life is meaningless we do not reach this conclusion by applying to his life our own personal standards. We do so by applying the standards of the person himself. Now, you'll ask, how is this possible? My reply is simple: by showing that his conviction that his life is meaningful or worthwhile is the product of self deception. Similarly, when a person, looking back at a period of his life, says his life was meaningless or worthless then, what he is saying is that at that earlier time, he was the victim of self deception. Furthermore, these references to self deception can be substantiated. When we say that a person's life is not meaningful to him, even when he does not recognize this, what we mean is that his life does not really mean very much to him, even though he thinks it does, and that his life and personality will have certain characteristics which support this judgment.

You can see how this avoids the paradox you were led into. My arguments enable us to preserve the undeniable variety of meanings which people find in life. On the other hand, they also enable one to say that a man's life is meaningless even when he does not recognize this, without imposing one's own standards of what is meaningful and worthwhile on to that life. One is enabled to say this by showing on the basis of evidence drawn from the life of the person we are considering, that he doesn't really see any meaning in or care for the things he says he cares for and finds meaningful. So where is your paradox now?

Agatharchus: It is true that you have removed the paradoxical conclusions which were bothering Callias, but only at a price. Your conclusions apply to some situations, but not to others. Yet, you have presented your arguments as if they applied generally. You have suggested that it would mean nothing to say that a person's life is meaningless or worthless unless you could show that the person himself, although he doesn't realize it, finds little meaning or worth in the life he is living. What I am saying is that this is unsatisfactory as a general thesis, simply because it applies to some cases, but not to others. The kind of example which the analysis fits might be as follows: A person says that money and prestige are the most important things in life, but things are not what they seem. The person concerned had been a student with a strong desire to become a teacher of English literature. Due to some financial trouble, however, he is forced to give up his studies. He works ruthlessly in business, becoming more and more successful, and the envy of many; the self-made man who once had nothing, now appears to have everything. He pours scorn on his former dreams as a student: those were days when he did not realize what made the world go round. But we feel that he is not behind his words. There is a desperation in the way he wants to tell everyone that he is now concerned with what really matters. We feel that his heart is not in his work, although (or perhaps because) he drives himself so relentlessly and unsparingly. It is evident that he still cares for what he calls a worthless dream. So when he tells us that money and prestige are the most important things in life, we say that he is deceiving himself. We say that we can support our conclusion by referring to his hopes, fears, desires, etc., and by telling the kind of story I have just outlined.

I'm saying that your answer to Callias fits the kind of case I have just described. But there are other cases which it does not fit at all. I'm thinking of the sense in which Socrates says in the *Gorgias* that the unjust man *cannot* be happy. This judgment seems to be unconditional. It certainly does not seem to wait on what the unjust man happens to want or think worthwhile. On the contrary, *despite* what he wants or thinks worthwhile, Socrates would say his life is meaningless. Furthermore, there is no suggestion that before Socrates can pass judgment on the unjust man, he must ensure that the unjust man has been dimly aware, at some time or other, that his life is meaningless. Even if it could be shown that the unjust man had never been aware, dimly or otherwise, of this fact, that would not deter Socrates from making his judgment. Think how strange it would be, Semeias, if we tried to express Socrates's judgment of Archelaus the tyrant of Macedonia in terms of your arguments. Socrates wants to say that Archelaus is not happy, that his life is devoid of meaning. But according to you, whether Socrates's suspicions are well-founded or not, what Socrates must be suspecting is that Archelaus, whether he recognizes it or not, does not think that his life means very much to him, and that his life and personality will bear marks of this. But this analysis simply obscures the nature of Socrates's judgment.

Polus tells us that Archelaus is among the happiest of men. This is what Archelaus himself might say. Socrates does not deny any of that, but he makes a moral judgment about it in terms of which Archelaus is seen as the unhappiest of men. What we have here are not suspicions awaiting confirmation in what the person condemned says or thinks about them, but an unconditional judgment which does not depend on the actual or possible assent of the person judged for its intelligibility.

Semeias: This seems too sudden to me. You speak as though nothing more can be said. I am suggesting, on the other hand, that before one can say a man is living for worthless things, one must have some evidence or proof from the man's life to support one's judgment. People find different things to be meaningful. What right have we to rule any out? We can only do so when, as you said, things are not what they seem. This was true of your example of the successful business man, whose whole hectic career was an attempt to hide from himself his longing for early interests which he never fulfilled. I'm suggesting that something similar *must* be true of Archelaus. His life too is an attempt to stave something off, perhaps the anguish and depression in his own heart.

Agatharchus: But how do you know this? It may or may not be the case that Archelaus's life is an attempt to stave off something. Surely, one can imagine someone living like Archelaus without attempting to stave off anything. Couldn't a man live for the kinds of things Archelaus lived for, not because he needed those things to stave off anything else, but simply because those were the things he wanted to live for? How can you argue that if a man lives the kind of life Archelaus lived self deception *must* be present? But what sort of a 'must' is this? Is it not a piece of philosophical legislation which falsifies the facts and obscures possibilities? The only reason you could have for saying that such characteristics must be present is that you are wedded to a philosophical *theory* about judgments concerning the meaning of life. One is then led to say, that if anyone recognizes that his life is meaningless, the recognition must involve locating features of his life *prior* to the recognition which show that he did not see a great deal of meaning in his life even then. What we see happening here is a philosophical theory determining our reading of the facts.

Semeias: All right, but I think more can be said. Without disputing your point, one might still argue that people who care little for moral considerations are alienated from themselves. Their lives will have certain divisive characteristics. The people concerned may not recognize these, but on the basis of them, one can say that they are deceiving themselves. The self-centred man is alienated from himself. Think of the man who wants to be well thought of by other people. It is easy to see how his egocentricity can lead to servility. In order to be well thought of by people of note he takes great pains to discover what pleases these people, what their opinions are, how to win their friendship and so on. Thus, he becomes servile in his attempt to secure prestige for himself. Self-centredness seems to lead to a man being at variance with himself. So if someone asks why we say that his life has little meaning or is the product of self deception, we can point to this fact as evidence or proof.

Agatharchus: But you are assuming that this fact is always present. You say: Show me a self-centred man, and I'll show you servility. The fact is that this is true of some forms of self-centredness, but not of all. Think of Al Capone.[1] Here, too, is a man who wanted to secure a place in the sun for himself, but he did so, not by becoming servile to those who already had such a place, but by seeing to it that he had the most prominent place of all. One might say that Al Capone pursued his ruthless policies with single-mindedness. It would simply be a distortion of the facts to describe Al Capone as someone whose life exhibited an inherent divisiveness. This being so, the attempt to show in any *general* way, why one should pay any attention to moral considerations, by appealing to the effects on one's personality, collapses.

Semeias: I still think that you are ignoring the possibility of some kind of psychological proof which would show that the man who strives to be decent is a happier and more integrated person than the man who has no time for moral considerations.

Agatharchus: Even if it were true that an integration of character were achieved as a result of heeding moral considerations, this fact would not illustrate the importance of such considerations. Furthermore, you assume that once a person has had the consequences of his evil ways pointed out to him, he will turn from

[1] The use made of this example was suggested to me by Mr H. O. Mounce.

his evil ways. But might not someone think his evil ways
are worth the trouble? Might he not recognize that he
could have been happier, and that his present life has
thwarted certain activities, and yet still feel that his
present life is infinitely more important than those other
things? Doesn't this apply to many dictators?

Semeias: I suppose what I am suggesting is that it ought
to be possible to show that a person who commits evil
deeds isn't really behind his actions. I'm suggesting
that this is involved in the very nature of evil actions.

Agatharchus: But this has yet to be established. Why
should the despicable deeds a person does be any less
a part of him than his good deeds? I agree that you
might be able to show in specific cases that a person
did not really care for his evil deeds, that these deeds
are not what they seem. But if it is possible for a person not to be behind his evil deeds, it is also possible
for a person to be behind his evil deeds. So whatever
is meant by saying that evil doing always involves an
alienation of the self, it cannot mean that a man is
never fully involved in the evil he does.

Semeias: If you say this, you seem to be left with the
problem with which Callias began the discussion. He
was worried by his failure to say what we are doing
when we say that a man's life is meaningless or worthless. For good reasons, he wanted to avoid imposing
his conceptions of what is important on to other
people's lives, and yet, on some occasions, he wanted
to say, 'A man who lives for those kinds of things is
leading a meaningless life.' In my first remarks, I
suggested that this latter judgment is possible only
when we can show that the person referred to is in

the grip of self deception. You have to show, for example, that the man who cares little for moral considerations is deceiving himself. Otherwise, how can
you call his life meaningless?

Agatharchus: I realize why you have argued in this
way, but I think it confuses matters. In fact, I think
your argument leads to a contradiction. Let us consider a pretty uncontroversial example of wilful pretence, namely, Uriah Heep's pretence at humility.
Now when Uriah Heep acted as he did, in what sense
can we say that he was deceived? The most natural
retort would be to say that far from being deceived,
he was doing the deceiving. But you want to say that
in some sense Uriah Heep is morally deceived. But it
is hard to give this a natural context. If I heard that
someone was morally deceived, I might think that he
was mistaken about the moral issues involved in a
situation, or in the grip of self deception about his own
motives and actions. But, clearly, this is not what you
have in mind now. You seem to be saying that in so
far as Uriah Heep cared little for other people, he was
deceiving himself. But when you say he was deceiving himself, are you saying any more than that he
did not care for others? So the language of deception
is misleading in this context. The man who misuses
other people is not unaware of the promises he has
made to them, the loans he has received from them,
the confidences he has shared with them; it is not that
he shuts his eyes to what is there to be seen, but that
he does not care about what he does see. The language
of deception and lack of understanding may mislead
us here. There is a use of 'understanding' which is
synonymous with 'caring', 'loving', etc. Thus, it might

be said that only the humble man possesses understanding. Here, the understanding is inseparable from
humility, and is almost a synonym for it. When we
say that the man who lacks humility lacks understanding, we are saying that he lacks the understanding that humility brings, which is a roundabout way of
repeating the assertion that he is not humble. Now in
another sense of 'understanding', a more familiar
one, Uriah Heep understands what humility is. If he
did not, he could not have deceived others about his
character. What he lacks is love for what he understands. Similarly, the priest and the levite who passed
by the bleeding wayfarer in the ditch on the road from
Jerusalem to Jericho understood the facts, they knew
he was there and that he was suffering. What they
lacked was pity and compassion. It was their hearts
and not their eyes which were shut to what they saw.

If you want to say more, if you want to say that
Uriah Heep is deceiving himself in the sense you have
been talking about it, then you do end up contra-
dicting yourself. On your view, Uriah Heep would be
deceiving himself if, without realizing it, he didn't
care for what he says he cares for. But as we have
seen, Uriah Heep is someone who has no consideration
for other people. If you call this self deception, you
have to say that really, Uriah Heep does care for
other people, since you'd have to show that his lack
of consideration is not what it seems. This is a blatant
contradiction.

Semeias: Yes, I see the difficulty.

Agatharchus: I can underline my point as follows. Let
us imagine that Uriah Heep or Archelaus in their old

age come to regret the way in which they have lived. Suppose they said that they had been deceiving themselves all that time. On your view, what this would amount to is that in their lives we could find signs that they did not really care for the things they said they cared for. One might say that Archelaus's life showed that he was frequently trying to stave off anguish and depression. One might say that there were some signs in Uriah Heep's life of melancholy when he put down a charitable impulse. All this might be true. But equally, it might not be true. I am thinking of Archelaus and Uriah Heep looking back on their lives in which there are no such characteristics. The character of the remorse they now feel would depend on that. Their reflections would not reveal such a terrible pattern if it could be shown that from time to time they had mourned or become depressed by a lost goodness in youth. But the truth I am imagining them as having to face up to is the fact that they had not mourned a lost goodness at any time, that they had felt no guilt.

Callias: Even if Semeias has no answer to you at the moment, I am not completely satisfied with what you say. You have argued that it is possible to pass certain kinds of moral judgments on the things people live for, without having to show that those people, in their heart of hearts as it were, really did not care very much for those things. In other words, you have argued that we can call a man's life meaningless without showing that that man is deceiving himself.

I should like to challenge your conclusion in this way: Think of a man who reforms, that is, a man who begins to pay attention to moral considerations.

What are we to say about the relation between the two periods in his life? There must be some connection between them. Indeed, I'm suggesting that there must be some features of his life in the earlier period which explain the *possibility* of the change which takes place later. I should like to mention four possibilities and to have your comments on them.

Let us take as our example a man who has lived most of his life thinking that money and prestige were the only things worth bothering about. Late in his life, during an illness, responding to the care and attention given to him by his family, he comes to see all he has not been and ought now to strive for. What makes such a change possible? The first possibility is the one you have discussed at length with Semeias. Might it not be the case that we find that this person had not really cared for money and prestige, even at the time when he did not recognize this? Even at that time, he really wanted what he arrives at late in life. Thus, when he does come to love others and forget himself, we can see that it had been possible for him, since this is really what he had wanted all along. What do you say to this?

Agatharchus: Let me make it quite clear that I do not deny that all you describe could be the case. All I am saying is that it needn't be true in order for a man to change his life radically in the way I have described. No such features as you mention need be present in his life before the change. At the end of his life, he may come to something which is new to him, something that he discovers for the first time, not something that he has wanted all along. Indeed, his shame

H

at his earlier life is due to the fact that he had not wanted this, but other things, all along.

Callias: Consider another suggestion. Might we not say that if it is to be possible for a man to change in the way we have described, it must be possible to prove to that man, before he changes, why he ought to change? For example, it might be possible to show that this man's greed for money and prestige led to a lot of trouble in his life: trouble in his marriage, in his professional life, in his friendships, and so on. What he comes to recognize late in life, on the other hand, brings him peace: peace in his family relationships, in his attitude to his professional career, and even peace in face of death. Thus, since one way of life brought him peace and the other brought him trouble, one way of life has been shown to be worthwhile and the other not.

Agatharchus: Your argument is fallacious. It suggests that the achievement of peace is an end to which *either* way of life could be a means. If this were true, the achievement of peace would be an external measure for assessing various ways of living. But the peace achieved at the end of his life by the man you described is not external to what he came to recognize. On the contrary, the peace can only be understood in terms of it. It is the peace which is bound up with loving others and forgetting himself. Thus, when he says that his earlier life is meaningless, he is making a judgment from within the moral perspective that he has embraced. He has not assessed that perspective in terms of any external measure. The temptation to think so may have been encouraged by the fact that in your example the moral perspective you described *did* bring peace to the person concerned. But one should not overlook the fact that the lives of people struggling to be faithful to such a perspective, need not be characterized by peace. Their lives may be a constant struggle against doubt and temptation. But they would not say that such struggling and striving are worthless even if the peace they seek is not in fact attained. Again, the temptation to talk as you did would be lessened if it were recognized that the man could have embraced a moral perspective which by its very nature did not bring peace to its adherents— for example, a reaction of rebellion and protest. Here, there would not be much sense in talking of his change of life as a means of securing peace.

Furthermore, the kind of perspective you talked of cannot be attained if it is pursued for any external reason. Humility cannot be made a means to anything without being destroyed. And that is a logical 'cannot'. If someone tried to emulate saintliness in order to forget some painful episodes in his life, for example, he would only attain a façade of saintliness.

When the man we are considering says his earlier life was meaningless, he does not mean that it is meaningless because it didn't work. At the end of his life, he says that his earlier life has been meaningless, and he says that it would have been meaningless even if he had died before his change of heart. So his reason for calling it meaningless, was not because it did not work, but because it was the kind of life it was. No matter how much success he had achieved in terms of it, his judgment would not have been different. For all these reasons, whatever might be meant by saying that it must have been possible for the man to change as he did, we cannot mean that it must be possible to provide an external justification of the moral perspective he came to embrace.

Callias: Perhaps my third possibility will fare better. Might it not be said that in order for a man to change in the way we have discussed, his earlier mode of life must contain the seeds of such change? This would apply to the case of self deception we have already considered, but the present suggestion is different. I have in mind the possibility of the person's prior mode of life having a parasitic or perverted character, in which case, one could imagine a person being weaned away from it by having the relation between his present way of life and that which it is parasitic on or a perversion of, made explicit. I have in mind someone who might want to say, like the Sophists in Plato's *Gorgias*, that it doesn't matter whether one says one thing rather than another: the best argument is the one that works and the best course of action is the one that succeeds. If this is put forward as an account of all that understanding and action involve, the irrationality of such an account could be pointed out. It could be shown that far from being an account of understanding and action, persuasion and manipulation of people's reactions are only possible where there is genuine understanding and action which cannot be understood in these terms. The perversion feeds on what is genuine.

Agatharchus: Once again, I would not want to deny the possibility of such a case. All I am denying is that it must be the case. A man's evil ways before his reform need not be a perversion of anything. If such a man is in the grip of the desire for esteem and admiration, this is one of the most primitive desires in human beings. It may be thought that the desire to be the centre of one's world, to excel, to be top, is only possible if the person concerned also has a genuine regard for something that is worthwhile *independently* of his excelling at it. But I believe this is a mistake. It is tempting to think that those who 'want to be top' acknowledge the ability of those who have reached the top, an acknowledgement which is independent of whether they in fact reach the top or not. This may be true of many people, but it needn't be true of the envious man I am considering. His attitude to those who have reached the top is sullied at its source: it takes the form not of admiration, but of envy. The possibility of his changing does not depend on his mode of life being parasitic or perverted.

Callias: My reaction to your rejection of the three possibilities I have mentioned as necessary conditions for the possibility of radical reform in a man's life, is to ask you to say what the necessary conditions are. Surely, there must be something which leads us to say that it must be possible for such a man to change. Perhaps my fourth and final suggestion will win your approval. Couldn't the possibility of the radical change we are talking about depend on the prior history of the person concerned in the sense that when the change occurs, it comes as no surprise to those who knew him? Consider the following case. Let us suppose that when the friends of Saint Paul heard about his conversion on the road to Damascus they said something like this: 'It comes as no surprise to us at all. Ever since that Christian Stephen was killed he has been on edge.

One could never mention the man's name to him without his losing his temper.' We would then say that although the change in Paul's life is said to begin at that time on the road to Damascus, it really began with his witnessing of Stephen's death. Thus we can locate features in Paul's life prior to his conversion, which lead us to recognize the possibility of that conversion before it actually occurred.

Agatharchus: There may be much to be said for the account of Paul's conversion which you have given. Nevertheless, there can be conversions to Christianity or to a variety of moral perspectives, which lack any evidence of the likelihood or possibility of such conversions prior to their occurrence. Instead of saying, as you imagined Paul's friends saying on hearing of his conversion, 'We could see it coming some time ago', people might say in reaction to an individual's conversion, 'He was the last person one would imagine such a thing happening to.'

You ask me to state what I think are the necessary conditions for radical change of the kind we have mentioned to take place in a person's life. I feel like saying that in order for such a change to be *possible*, nothing more is needed than that the person should be in a state other than the one he attains. Because the state a person is in is different from the moral perspective he embraces later, he can be changed or converted to it. But I do not think one can legislate on how such changes come about. Sometimes they are gradual, sometimes sudden. Sometimes there are features in a person's life prior to his conversion, which made the conversion an expected event. But this need not be the case always. So the first condition which is necessary for there to be a change, is simply that the person is in a state, which, from a certain moral perspective, calls for change. Secondly, for a person to attain a new moral recognition, he must be in a society or be related to a society, in which such a recognition has meaning. Thus, what he comes to recognize is not something peculiar to himself. I do not see any point in speculating on precisely what must be true of people prior to the embracing of such a perspective in order that they might be converted. Sometimes, when people change, we can see in their previous ways of living, self deception, perversion or signs that a change of heart was on the way. But sometimes their lives contain no such features and they are as surprised by the change which overtakes them as anyone else.

Semeias: I think I see now why you were right in criticizing me earlier, when I said that one could only call a man's life meaningless or worthless if you could show that really he did not see very much meaning or worth in his life, even when he did not recognize this. What I was saying in effect was that such judgments must depend on proving that the person concerned was deceiving himself.

Agatharchus: Quite so. I have never denied that when people do look back over their lives, they may say that they have betrayed what they cared for most. The ruthless business man we considered might have said that. Or consider a man who is by nature extremely generous, but who, on a given occasion, gives money to an acquaintance knowing it will bring about his downfall, but deceives himself into thinking that he is being generous. There is the possibility here of showing him that he is deceiving himself, by locating features of his behaviour which show that although he did not realize it, he did not really care for the man he said he was helping. But I was considering the case of the man who never did care for anyone else, and who later changed his ways. When he says that his former life is meaningless, he does not mean that he betrayed what he cared for most. On the contrary, he calls it meaningless because what he cared for most was, say, money and prestige. So he cannot say that he was deceiving himself at that earlier time. If he was deceiving himself, his criteria of assessment would have to be the same for the two periods of his life. His judgment would then be based on the determination of a matter of fact. A man might have thought that he couldn't be happier and then later, when he has more money and prestige, he has to admit that he was wrong. But his conception of happiness remains unchanged. The case is very different, however, when a man says that he was wrong in thinking that his life was meaningful when he thought of nothing but money and prestige. If we want to speak of a conflict between this man's conceptions of happiness, it is very different from what is meant by conflict in our previous example, since *that* conflict depended on the concept of happiness remaining unchanged. Something that was asserted of an earlier period is now denied. But the other man who says that he has lived a meaningless life, does not deny that from the point of view of a certain conception of happiness he had been happy; what he does is to call that conception of happiness a false one. He does not deny that he had been happy when he thought little of moral considerations, but now that he has come to see the importance of those considerations, he calls his previous happiness worthless.

What I am insisting on is the possibility of calling a certain conception of happiness false, where this in no way implies the possibility of any kind of *proof* of the falsity in terms of what the person judged really wants. There is no common measure between the two conceptions of happiness whereby the first can be shown to be mistaken. For lack of regard and regard for moral considerations there is no system which includes both. How then can we speak of the former as a deception or a delusion?

Semeias: I thought you would argue in that way, and I agree with much of what you say. Nevertheless, I think you are wrong when you conclude that it cannot be said that the man who lives for money and prestige is deceiving himself. I want to show why you come to this false conclusion.

Earlier, you argued that I was wrong in insisting that whenever we say that a man's life is meaningless, it must be possible to show that the person concerned does not really care for what he says he cares for. You also said I was wrong to insist that in calling the life of the man who cared little for moral considerations meaningless, it must be possible to show that, despite appearances, he really cared for moral considerations. I came to see that I was wrong. I realize that what held me captive was a too narrow conception of what judgments concerning the meaning of life might mean. But haven't you now fallen into a similar trap?

Agatharchus: What do you mean?

Semeias: You are prepared to say that you can call the life of a man who lives for money and prestige meaningless, without the kind of proof I argued for at the outset. You showed me that 'meaningless' can be used as a moral judgment. The life judged is called meaningless, not because it is not what it seems, but precisely because it is the kind of life it is. But you are not prepared to say that the man who lived such a life is deceiving himself, without the kind of proof which, in the case of judgments of meaninglessness, you said was not necessary. But just as I had too narrow a view of judgments of meaninglessness, you have too narrow a view of self deception.

Agatharchus: My difficulty is to see how a man can be said to have been deceiving himself in an earlier way of life, when there is a radical discontinuity between it and his present way of life.

Semeias: But the discontinuity and radical opposition of his way of life before and after his reform, are precisely what enable us to speak of self deception here. Consider the two statements, 'I was wrong to have given assistance to that young poet' and 'I was wrong when I said that money and prestige were all that mattered.' What does 'wrong' come to here? In the first statement, within the standards of worthiness recognized and used by the benefactor, 'wrong' could be replaced by 'mistaken' without loss of meaning. The benefactor thought that the poet was going to fulfil certain expectations, but he failed to do so. By poets unworthy of assistance, he means, in fact, those

who do not or could not be expected to fulfil such
expectations. Therefore, he concludes, he was wrong
to assist the poet. The benefactor has not changed his
conception of what is worth supporting. He is, in this
respect, the same kind of person at the time when he
recognizes his mistake as he was at the time that he
made his original judgment. His change of opinion
is not a change in him. But now consider the case of
a man who says that he has been wrong in devoting
his life to seeking prestige and making money. Why
can't we say here that he has simply made a mistake,
a mistake about what is important in life? The trouble
with this is that it may lead us to construe 'mistake'
as we did in our previous example, and that would be
to ignore a feature of the present case. When a person comes to see that he has been wrong in devoting
his life to seeking prestige, etc., it is not as if his
criteria of what is important remain the same—it is
not as if he recognizes that he has made a mistake in
the given instance, so remaining essentially the same
kind of person. On the contrary, the change I have
referred to involves a change in the person. It is not
simply that his opinions change; *he* changes. Thus, the
self is central in the second example. And when such
a change occurs, it is perfectly natural for the person
to express it by saying that he had been deceiving
himself when he thought that money and prestige
were the most important things in life. If we want to
say he was mistaken, we must remember that in this
context 'mistake' can be equated with delusion; that
is what being mistaken comes to here.

Agatharchus: Yes, you are right. I was so anxious to
distinguish between such cases as you have outlined

and those in which self deception involves showing
that someone did not really care for what he thought
he cared for, that I ruled out the possibility of calling
the former cases instances of self deception. I see now
that our use of 'self deception' is more varied than I
had supposed. I would want to say, however, that in
order to distinguish between the two cases we've just
been discussing, it is absolutely vital to stress that the
man who confesses that he was deceived in thinking
that money and prestige were the most important
things in life, is the object and not the agent of the
deception. I realize that it might be asked, in that case,
who deceives him. But couldn't we say that money
and prestige deceive him? It might be said that money
and prestige in themselves can't deceive anyone; they
have to become entangled with the souls of men. This
indeed is true, but it ignores the status enjoyed by
money and prestige in human life. Of course, it is true
that were it not for men's doings, they could not have
that status, but, nevertheless, the status cannot be
explained purely in terms of the intentions of any
individual or group of individuals. Economic, political,
social, cultural and religious factors can nourish that
status. This is part of the reason why we speak of the
snares of this life as an evil greater than ourselves.

Semeias: I agree with all you say, but it is still inadequate. Now you appreciate that the variety involved in our use of 'self deception' was greater than
you thought you are in danger still of obscuring a
parallel variety in the use of the expression, 'I was
deceiving myself.' What you say makes the self look
too much like a passive recipient. There *is* a need to
say that the self is the agent as well as the object of

the deception. For once a person has been attracted
by money and prestige in the way I have indicated,
he makes those aims his own, they become part of
him, they determine the nature of his hopes and fears,
his conceptions of what is important, his assessment
of people, etc. etc. He perpetuates and generates the
deception in his own life. Thus, when a person comes
to see this period of his life as a delusion, he can
say, with good reason, not simply, 'I was deceived,'
but also, 'I was deceiving myself.'

Agatharchus: Yes, I take your point. In the light of it,
I think we are also in a better position to appreciate
the meaning of expressions like 'one's better self',
'one's true self', 'betraying one's true self', etc. In the
way you argued at first in this discussion, if someone
said that a man who thought money and prestige
were the most important things in life betrayed his
true self, he would mean that one could show that the
man did not really care for money and prestige,
though he thought he did. Thus, in giving his time
and energy to these things, he betrayed what he cared
for most. Similarly, in saying that he had come to
himself, he would be saying that he had come to
recognize what he had really cared for all along. That
was your earlier position. But although this corre-
sponds to some cases, you and I now agree that it
obscures other possibilities. Think of the Parable of
the Prodigal Son. We are told that having left home
and squandered all that he had, he came to himself,
and said, 'I will arise, and go to my father.' Now, in
saying this, no moral notions need be involved. I have
heard people say of a husband who returned to his
wife after a separation, 'He came to himself', and I

have understood what they meant when they added, 'He soon came to see on which side his bread was buttered.' It might have been like that in the case of the Prodigal Son. 'When he came to himself', might have meant no more than, 'When he saw what a fool he had been in not realizing when he was well off'. But that is not what *is* meant. The identity of the self to which he came is a moral identity, an identity bound up with the ideals of a filial relationship in a Jewish household. He had not wanted that all along; that is not what is meant by calling his giving himself to these ideals 'his true identity'. No, he had not wanted them. He had forsaken them completely for the sake of worldliness. In doing so, he was deceiving himself, and when he realized this his response was repentance, 'I am no longer worthy to be called thy son.' Of course, the parable is meant to show us something of God's relationship to men. For the believer, his identity, his true self, is bound up with the reality of God. The believer would say that this was his true identity even at the time when he was an atheist with no thought of God. So 'true identity' in this context cannot be equated with 'that which I have really cared for all along'. The Christian understanding of this fact is only one conception of 'true identity'. There are others, of course, rival religious or moral conceptions. But it is not the business of the philosopher as such to say that one conception is superior to the others.

Callias: Both of you seem to have reached an agreement and in doing so shed a lot of light on my initial puzzle. If I have understood your arguments, you have wanted to show the character of certain moral

judgments. You considered the example of a man who
lived for money and prestige. What you showed was
how it is possible for someone to say of such a man,
or how he can say of himself, that his life is meaningless, that he is deceiving himself, that he has betrayed
his better self, without any of this implying that his
regard for money and prestige is other than it seems.
On the contrary, the force of the judgments depend
on the regard being precisely what it seems to be. Was
that the burden of your arguments?

Semeias: Indeed it was.

Agatharchus: I agree, but there is one point I should
like to add. When we say that the happiness of a man
who lives for money and prestige is a false conception
of happiness, or when the man says this of an earlier
time in his own life, there is no question of proving the
falsity in terms of some common measure which the
two conceptions of happiness share. I stressed this
earlier. What I wish to add is that this does not mean
that nothing can be said about what the falsity involves. One can say a lot in making one's moral judgment more explicit; one can show what is involved in
it. What it is essential to note, however, is that in
doing this, one is not *proving* the falsity of the conception of happiness, but *elucidating* it, and this
elucidation is unintelligible apart from the moral
perspective from within which it is made.

CHAPTER 5

ALIENATION AND MORAL REGARD

İlham Dilman

> This above all: to thine own self be true,
> And it must follow, as the night the day,
> Thou canst not then be false to any man
> (*Hamlet*, Act I, Scene III).

I HAVE argued that words to this effect are often used to refer to a person's *moral* identity or autonomy. I suggested, however, that *more* may be claimed by such words as 'He has not been himself', 'He has not been true to himself'. This is what I was thinking of earlier when I spoke of the 'alienated character' of Ivan Ilych's life.[1] But the account I gave there of what this means was very inadequate.

When on his death-bed Ivan Ilych calls up in imagination the best moments of his life these strike him as absolutely different from what they had seemed to him at the time. The person who had enjoyed these best moments of his life now strikes him as almost a stranger—'it was as if it were the remembrance of someone else'. There was gaiety, friendship and hopes in his early youth, whereas his later life was filled with 'this dead service, and these labours for money'. Nothing new came into it—'one year, and two, and ten, and twenty,—and always the same thing. And

[1] See pp. 16 and 19 above.

the longer it went, the more dead it became.' For the most part his responses were not really his: they did not come from him. They were governed by his need for approval, by his conception of what was expected of him, and by considerations of gain. His concern with keeping up appearances, his concern with what those that mattered thought of him, gradually usurped the place of concern, passion and conviction.

Tolstoy speaks of Ivan Ilych having separated 'his real life from the official side of affairs' and goes on to show that this was equally true of his family life and marriage. There is nothing that one would call growth there; only the hardening of set responses. In fact, his reaction to any situation which demanded some genuine response from him was one of withdrawal. He tried to keep such demands at bay 'by the same easy and decorous relation to life that had served him heretofore'. When this failed, he 'transferred the centre of gravity of his life to his official work; he grew to like this work better and became more ambitious than before'. He did not like it for what he found in it, but because of what it did for him.

The possibility of growth in the various activities in which he engaged was stifled by his dependence on routine and ritual and by his egocentric ambitions. As this dependence grew and the dominion of his ambitions increased, his engagement in these activities became increasingly more tenuous. His participation became little more than going through the motions. His concern with the achievement of ends external to these activities made it impossible for him to find sustenance in them.

Briefly, then, his 'easy and decorous relation to life' had taken the place of any genuine response to

I

people and situations, and his concern with what this was to achieve for him replaced any genuine concern and interest he might have developed. He had separated his real life not only from his family life and the official side of affairs, but from pretty well everything he engaged in and did. In other words, he had lost his capacity to be himself both at home, at work, and in his social life. Instead he put on attitudes, was meticulous to do the done thing, the correct thing, to behave with decorum. This is what I mean by self alienation.

We all know what it is for a man not to be himself in a situation, to feel forced to put on an act—for instance, Bernard Shaw's Pygmalion during her first introduction to society. Normally this is not something that a man enjoys and he is glad to get out of such a situation. However, there are people who positively enjoy putting on an act. They seem to enjoy vicariously something not their own and they feel safe behind the act. It is, therefore, not surprising that they should seek situations which provide them with the opportunity to put on an act and cultivate certain attitudes. Obviously the more successful they are, the more they can charm, impress, manipulate people, or keep them at bay, the more the act and attitude will become second nature to them. As D. H. Lawrence once put it: 'With men and women everything is an attitude only when something else is lacking. Something is lacking and they are thrown back on their own devices.'[1]

It is not too difficult to see what Lawrence was thinking of here. We all know the difference, for instance, between a man whose anger is effective, who when offended can live his anger out, and a man whose anger is a learned reaction to cues and never finds a

[1] 'St Mawr', *The Tales of D. H. Lawrence*, pp. 566–7.

full blooded expression. The latter's anger is not something in front of which one flinches. What there is of it smoulders in secret resentment. Lawrence contrasts what he calls 'attitude' in men and women with the 'black fiery flow' in the eyes of St Mawr. He finds that 'terrifying and real'—something that you have to reckon with, something that you cannot manipulate or bend to your wishes. Professor Macmurray has said that there is 'a staleness and dullness' about the feelings of a man who is not himself—'as if the spirit of the man isn't in them'. 'He hasn't any real opinions of his own, they do not come out of his experience of life.' 'He is apt to be overlooked in company, as if he wasn't there. He tends to chatter a lot and thrust himself forward, but you feel that the energy is somehow worked up and galvanised into action. It isn't the spontaneous flowing out of a fund of life in him.' 'He lives on other people, reacting to them, stimulated into self assertion by them.'[1]

I doubt that such a man can be either good or evil —evil, for instance in the way that Iago was in contriving to bring about the downfall of Othello. His moral beliefs, his feelings for good and evil, his concern for other people, will be as unreal as his anger, his indignation, his outrage, or his enthusiasm. I doubt that his moral beliefs can *mean* more to him than his other concerns and activities.

Wittgenstein pointed out that a man's moral beliefs must be *his*, not just what he takes on trust.[2]

[1] *Freedom in the Modern World*, pp. 153–4.

[2] Waismann's 'Notes on Talks with Wittgenstein', *Philosophical Review*, January 1965: 'At the end of my lecture on ethics I spoke in the first person. I believe that is quite essential. Here nothing more can be established, I can only appear as a person speaking for myself.'

This does not mean that he must have good grounds for holding them if he is to have more than mere opinion on moral matters. The distinction between having made the moral beliefs by which one lives *one's own* and having second-hand opinions has nothing to do with grounds, but with whether or not one has genuine moral concern. One could put this by speaking of *subjectivity*, to emphasize that speaking and acting from moral conviction is incompatible with detachment. Detachment here is the antithesis of concern, and it is the latter which brings to a man's moral judgments and decisions that *impersonal* element without which we would speak of bias, insincerity and illusion. When I speak of subjectivity I am thinking of the way in which a moral judgment or decision inevitably involves the speaker or agent who makes the judgment or takes the decision, of how the moral beliefs in the framework of which he judges and acts sit in him. In other words, I am thinking of his relaion as an individual to the values in terms of which he makes up his mind on moral issues that confront him. These values are, of course, independent of his wishes and desires, and he comes into contact with them in the way that he comes into contact with much else in the life and culture of the community to which he belongs.

If, then, I make a moral judgment, that judgment has to come *from me*. If I leave myself out I would merely be reporting a judgment. Someone who heard me could justly retort: 'So that is not what *you* think.' If I had any thoughts on the matter, if for instance I believed that what someone did was a despicable thing to do, I could not say so and leave myself out of the picture. If I really think that what he did is despicable, I am responding to what he did. What we have here is *my* response. I could not, as with a scientific conclusion to which I am forced by experimental evidence, say that what I think is unimportant. If in the case of a moral judgment I leave out what *I* think we seem to be left with what is *considered* right or wrong, admirable or despicable. This is mere opinion, as opposed to conviction.

In *Beyond Good and Evil* Nietzsche spoke of 'the objective man'. He said: 'The objective man is in truth a mirror; accustomed to prostration before everything that wants to be known, with such desires only as knowing or "reflecting" imply.' Such a person, Nietzsche says, 'has come to regard himself as the passage or reflection of outside forms or events. He calls up the recollection of "himself" with an effort. He readily confounds himself with other persons. His mirroring and eternally self-polishing soul no longer knows how to affirm, no longer how to deny.' The kind of person Nietzsche is thinking of can, I suppose, make fine moral distinctions. But he does not or cannot respond to good and evil. Where he is drawn into a dispute he displays, perhaps, a dispassionate desire to do justice to the different points of view involved; he reflects them most sensitively. But, like a mirror, he has no point of view on the matter himself. That is why, I take it, Nietzsche calls him 'objective'. He does not take anyone's side; but he does not stand here as opposed to there, or there as opposed to here— he has no stand-point of his own.

Such a person would have nothing to *say*, nothing to contribute to a moral discussion. If one were morally perplexed, this is not the kind of person one would go to for help. One would have nothing to learn from him. For the kind of understanding that a moral agent has of the issues and situations that confront him and others depends largely on where he stands with regard to the norms of the moral practice to which he belongs. His relation to them, what they mean to him, the role they play in his life, is logically relevant to the significance of the conclusions he reaches and the actions he takes on their basis.

Thus the growth of moral understanding involves more than the mere learning of moral standards and the ability to participate intelligently in the moral practice to which these standards belong. It involves coming to have regard for them, and this is a change in the person—a change in his relations with other people, a change in his attitude in a great many situations. In the case of Kitty Scherbatsky coming to have regard for the values she had learned from her parents in her childhood was a growth of wisdom. It is because the growth of virtue and wisdom involves an inner transformation, because the ignorance, mistakes, prejudices and illusions which moral education has to remove or dispel involve the self, that both Plato and Wittgenstein doubted that virtue and wisdom can be taught.[1]

Of the man who has no feeling for the standards of the moral practice to which he belongs we would say: 'He knows what others call "good", what people

---

[1] Both were certain that these cannot be imparted by training and instruction, that they cannot be imposed on a person, like many other forms of knowledge: the person has to come to them himself. The impetus for the growth of virtue and wisdom can only come from a person's own life—always remembering that the possibilities contained there are dependent on the culture and traditions within which he lives, thinks and feels.

consider "right". That is all. The values by which he acts and lives are not his values; he has not made them his own.' From him we would expect, perhaps, the voicing of popular opinion or a conventional judgment; but no real understanding of our difficulties. Thus it is not only *what* moral beliefs a man holds that is relevant to the moral significance of what he says and does, but also *how* he holds them.

I suggested that indifference to good and evil is one form of alienation that necessarily involves the self. There is a close parallel between the moral life of such a person and the life of a man who is not himself. I had said that the man who is not himself has nothing to say, nothing to give. The man who has not made his own the values which govern his actions has nothing to say either—on moral questions. Such a man need not be otherwise dead or hollow. But the reverse does not hold: A man who had lost his capacity to be himself is bound to be morally and spiritually dead.

> Under the brown fog of a winter dawn,
> A crowd flowed over London Bridge, so many,
> I had not thought death had undone so many.
> > T. S. Eliot, *The Waste Land*

Such a man can call nothing his own—neither his values, nor the emotions he displays, the desires he seeks to satisfy, the interests he pursues, the actions he performs, the activities in which he engages. He is Kafka's 'complete citizen' who 'travels over the sea in a ship with foam before him and wake behind, that is, with much effect round about'. Kafka said of him that 'he and his property are not one but two, and whoever destroys the connection destroys him at the same time'.[1] We can see this in the case of Ivan Ilych. His self confidence depended on his success, on his obtaining the esteem and approval of others. Any situation that threatened to take these things away from him left him with the feeling that he had nothing to fall back on and so filled him with the terror of annihilation.

It was this that I had mostly in mind when I asked in what sense Ivan Ilych's life had been meaningless. What I had not recognized then was how a person could be indifferent to good and evil, and in this sense be said to have betrayed his true or better self, without in any other way being alienated from himself. If such a man's life could be said to bear the marks of his moral and spiritual alienation this would involve a moral judgment.

What this whole discussion has brought to light is the *variety* to be found in the judgments we make when we question the sense of a person's life, when we say that someone is deceiving himself, and when we say that he is not himself or that he has been untrue to himself, and the way in which much of what we are thinking here cannot be understood in purely psychological terms.

[1] *Diaries*, vol. I, 1910–13.

BIBLIOGRAPHY

Works Cited

DOSTOEVSKY, Fyodor: *The Brothers Karamazov*, trans. by Constance Garnett, Everyman's Library, 1957

—— *The Devils*, trans. by David Magarshack, The Penguin Classics

—— *The Eternal Husband*, trans. by Constance Garnett, William Heinemann, 1950

ELIOT, T. S.: *The Cocktail Party*, London, Faber, 1950

—— 'The Waste Land', *Collected Poems 1909–1962*, London, Faber, 1963

FLEW, A. G. N.: 'Tolstoy and the Meaning of Life', *Ethics*, January 1963

HEPBURN, Ronald: 'Questions about the Meaning of Life', *Religious Studies*, April 1968

KAFKA, Franz: *Diaries*, Vol. I, 1910–13, ed. by Max Brod, London, Secker & Warburg, 1948

KIERKEGAARD, Søren: *Purity of Heart*, trans. by Douglas Steere, Fontana Books, 1961

LAWRENCE, D. H.: 'St Mawr', *The Tales of D. H. Lawrence*, Secker, 1934

MACMURRAY, John: *Freedom in the Modern World*, Faber Papercover edition

MARCEL, Gabriel: 'The Ego and Its Relation to Others', *Homo Viator*, Victor Gollancz, 1951

MARQUAND, John P.: *H. M. Pulham Esq.*, London, Hale, 1942

NIETZSCHE, Friedrich: *Beyond Good and Evil*, ed. by Oscar Levy, trans. by Helen Zimmern, London and Edinburgh, Foulis, 1909

PLATO: *Gorgias*, The Penguin Classics

—— *Symposium*, The Penguin Classics

—— *Crito*, *The Last Days of Socrates*, The Penguin Classics

—— *The Republic*, Everyman's Library, 1950

REICH, Wilhelm, *The Sexual Revolution*, Vision Press, 1969

RHEES, Rush: 'Wittgenstein's Builders', *Aristotelian Society, Proceedings*, 1959–60

STOCKS, J. L.: *Morality and Purpose*, ed. with an Introduction by D. Z. Phillips, Routledge & Kegan Paul, 1969

TOLSTOY, Leo: 'The Death of Ivan Ilych', *The Death of Ivan Ilych and Other Stories*, trans. by Aylmer Maude, Signet Classic, The New American Library, 1960

—— 'Father Sergius', *The Kreutzer Sonata and Other Stories*, trans. by Aylmer Maude, World's Classics, Oxford University Press, 1960

—— *Anna Karenina*, trans. by Rosemary Edmunds, The Penguin Classics

—— *A Confession*, trans. by Aylmer Maude, World's Classics, Oxford University Press, 1961

WAISMANN, Friedrich: 'Notes on Talks with Wittgenstein', *Philosophical Review*, January 1965

WEIL, Simone: *The Need for Roots*, trans. by A. F. Wills, Routledge & Kegan Paul, 1952

—— *Gravity and Grace*, trans. by Emma Craufurd, Routledge & Kegan Paul, 1952

—— *Waiting on God*, trans. by Emma Craufurd, Fontana Books, 1959

WINCH, Peter: *Moral Integrity*, Blackwell, 1968

WISDOM, John: 'What is there in Horse Racing?', *Listener*, 10 June 1954

WITTGENSTEIN, Ludwig: *Tractatus Logico-Philosophicus*, trans. by D. F. Pears and B. F. McGuinness, Routledge & Kegan Paul, 1961

—— 'A Lecture on Ethics', *Philosophical Review*, January 1965

—— *Lectures and Conversations on Aesthetics, Psychology and Religious Belief*, ed. by Cyril Barrett, Basil Blackwell, 1966

—— *Philosophical Investigations*, Blackwell, 1953

—— *Remarks on the Foundations of Mathematics*, Basil Blackwell, 1956

Works of Reference Not Cited

ANDERSON, John: 'Freudianism and Society', *Studies in Empirical Philosophy*, Angus and Robertson, 1962

FOOT, Philippa: 'Moral Beliefs', *Aristotelian Society, Proceedings*, 1958

HOLLAND, R. F.: 'Morality and the Two Worlds Concept', *Aristotelian Society, Proceedings*, 1955–6

MERTON, Thomas: *Seeds of Contemplation*, London: Hollis and Carter, 1956

PHILLIPS, D. Z. and MOUNCE, H. O.: *Moral Practices*, Routledge & Kegan Paul, 1970

RHEES, Rush: 'Some Developments in Wittgenstein's View of Ethics', *Philosophical Review*, January 1965

SOPHOCLES: 'Antigone', *The Theban Plays*, trans. by E. F. Watling, The Penguin Classics

WEIL, Simone: 'God in Plato', *On Science, Necessity and the Love of God*, Oxford University Press, 1968

WINCH, Peter: 'Can a Good Man be Harmed?', *Aristotelian Society, Proceedings*, 1965–6

WISDOM, John: 'Gods', *Philosophy and Psycho-Analysis*, Basil Blackwell, 1953

—— *Paradox and Discovery*, Basil Blackwell, 1965

INDEX

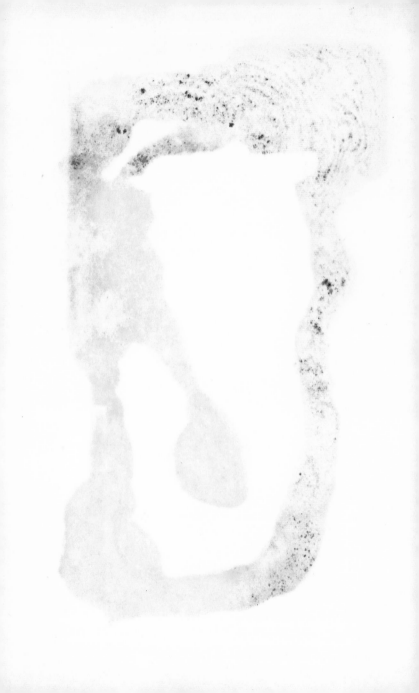